Twenty-Four

Twenty-Four

Integrating faith and real life

Krish Kandiah

LONDON ● ATLANTA ● HYDERABAD

Copyright © 2007 Krish Kandiah

12 11 10 09 08 07 06   7 6 5 4 3 2 1

First published 2007 by Authentic Media
9 Holdom Avenue, Bletchley, Milton Keynes, MK1 1QR, UK
285 Lynnwood Avenue, Tyrone, GA 30290, USA
OM Authentic Media, Medchal Road, Jeedimetla Village,
Secunderabad 500 055, A.P., India
www.authenticmedia.co.uk
Authentic Media is a division of Send the Light Ltd., a company limited
by guarantee (registered charity no. 270162)

British Library Cataloguing in Publication Data
A catalogue record for this book is available from the
British Library

ISBN-13: 978-1-85078-729-7
ISBN-10: 1-85078-729-8

Cover Design by fourninezero design.
Print Management by Adare Carwin
Printed in Great Britain by J.H. Haynes & Co., Sparkford

Contents

Contents

Thanks

I would like to thank my Christian family at Elmfield who first inspired these chapters to be preached. Thank you also to the following friends who helped with the preparation of these pages: James Ayrton, Graham Brown, Kim Hubbard and Professor Alister McGrath. I would like to especially thank my wife Miriam who was invaluable in the writing of this book and to my children Joel, Luke and Anna for encouraging me in my faith.

Introduction

My favorite television show is *24*. It traces in real time the adventures of Jack Bauer, the finest field agent at the Counter Terrorism Unit of the American Government. The show has a cult following: it is a riveting program and many of my friends have been known to watch multiple episodes back to back, losing many hours of sleep in the process. I must admit that I have acquired not only several of the DVD sets, but also the CTU ring tone for my mobile phone.

Jack Bauer is many people's idea of the ultimate hero. In each episode, we shadow him as he makes decisions that affect world security. In the 120 hours we have seen of Jack's life so far, we have watched him handle grief and joy, romance, back-biting at the office and substance addiction recovery. We have seen him kill hundreds of bad guys, rescue the US president on numerous occasions and save the world six times. (Incidentally he has never needed the toilet, gone home to bed, had a meal sitting down or run out of batteries on his mobile phone.) Jack Bauer packs a lot into a day. He is driven by allegiance to his country and a concern for national security; Jack is not a part-time agent – he's full on twenty-four hours a day.

In contrast, many Christians live as though their faith were a part-time commitment. We often settle for a spirituality restricted to Bible study and church services, which means that we live most of our lives without reference to God. We become professing Christians but practising atheists. But Christians are called to worship God with every breath they take and every moment of their lives. What we need is a way of integrating our faith into our daily lives and worshipping God through all that we do.

This book will help us to find ways of relating our faith to the whole of life, by shadowing an average Christian over twenty-four hours and considering how life and faith can be integrated. We look during the course of this twenty-four hours at everyday activities, including commuting, shopping and cooking and learn that God has designed each one of them to be both a way to serve him and a way to draw closer to him. This is the highest calling that we have.

Each chapter will look at an area of life within the broad sweep of the Bible's story in the hope that a passion for God will ignite our hearts and transform our everyday experiences to God-centered living. Each chapter contains a number of practical and creative suggestions, which I also aspire to put into practice. These suggestions will help us to redeem each activity and to practise true spirituality, bringing glory to the God we pledge allegiance to, twenty-four hours a day.

GET UP

A FRESH START

A wake-up call

When I was a teenager, my best mate Simon and I were heavily into computers; in fact if there had been a magazine called *Geek Weekly*, we would have been avid subscribers. We used to hang out after school, getting quite worked up about which of us had the best bit of IT kit. Today an electronic toaster probably has more processing power than the bits of technology we used to argue over. Naturally I always won the best computer competition, and Simon would exact his revenge by cunningly hiding my alarm clock. I would go to sleep dreaming about ram chips and floppy disk drives, only to be woken at 2 a.m. by my sabotaged time piece, hidden somewhere under mounds of wires, books and clothes, with no hope of finding it. All I could do was pray the batteries would run out soon.

My children have been an excellent alarm clock ever since they came into the world; unfortunately not the sort you can program. Again I was awake at 2 a.m. for no apparent reason. I lived for many years in a state of permanent sleep deprivation. I was always dressed and fiddling with Lego before 7.30 a.m. and I was never late for work. Incoherent and half-dazed perhaps, but not late.

Whether it's the shrill alarm of our personally programed acoustic time bomb, the heart-rending cry of a baby, the clattering of the dustbins, the sun's rays or the cat's nuzzling, we all have a daily prompt that activates us out of our sweet slumber and the warm confines of our duvets. Some of us manage it with a stretch, others with a struggle. Some of us need a shout, others need a shower. Most of us need coffee. Before we get locked into the routine of the day, let us reflect on those moments between our bedclothes and our work clothes. These moments of transition can be significant. Considering what motivates our first steps of the day could be the first step in learning how we can live every moment for God and how we can worship him twenty-four hours a day. The Bible calls us to wake up to certain realities, promises and challenges when we are getting started for the day.

Waking up and God's grace

He was on the run. He had major family problems. His own son had turned against him. To make matters worse, his son was in control of the country and had commissioned the army to track him down and kill him. The army was close on his trail.

This was the most unlikely setting for worship. Yet somehow in the middle of this crisis, King David found both the time and the inclination to compose a worship song.

> O LORD, how many are my foes!
> How many rise up against me!
> Many are saying of me,
> "God will not deliver him."
> But you are a shield around me, O LORD;
> you bestow glory on me and lift up my head.
> To the LORD I cry aloud,
> and he answers me from his holy hill.
> I lie down and sleep;
> I wake again, because the LORD sustains me.
> I will not fear the tens of thousands
> drawn up against me on every side.
> Arise, O LORD!
> Deliver me, O my God!
> Strike all my enemies on the jaw;
> break the teeth of the wicked.
> From the LORD comes deliverance.
> May your blessing be on your people

(Ps. 3:1-8).

he doesn't worry he knows God is in control of the situation + he knows what is best

Give God credit for what he has done! Don't just think things happen due to fate - know it is God!

David is wide awake to the gravity of his situation. With eyes open, he opens his heart too and cries out to God over the apparent hopelessness of his circumstances. He has more enemies than he can count and, according to the rumours, he has got himself into a hole that even God can't rescue him from. Yet David refuses to let adversity have the final say on his soul. David voices his cry to God and is then able to sleep, even though there is a search and destroy mission closing down on him. When David wakes up again, he knows it is due to God's direct intervention. From the moment of waking, he is conscious of God's protecting love around him.

Most of us do not go to sleep with the same threat of imminent death hanging over us. However, for many of us the weight of family and work problems are very present at bedtime. Often getting up again in the morning to face those same pressures can feel like we are up against a firing squad. We need to learn from David's perspective of seeing the day ahead as a grace gift from God, no matter what we face when we wake up.

I was reading recently about the famous flautist James Galway who narrowly escaped death in a horrendous car accident. He was interviewed shortly afterwards and asked what difference it was going to make to his life. He answered that because he had come so close to death, he had realised that life was precious, and could be snatched away in an instant. He was determined that every performance from then on would be given as if it were his last. Every concert and every CD was going to get all he had got. He understood the mercy of being granted a bit longer on this earth. Sometimes it takes a near death experience to make us realise the value of life. If, like David, we can understand each new day as a merciful gift from God, this will radically reorient the way that we face each new morning we are given.

There is a verse in Paul's letter to church in Rome that is particularly helpful in this: "Therefore brothers, I urge you, in view of God's mercy, to offer your bodies as living sacrifices – this is your spiritual act of worship" (Rom. 12:1). The verse is pivotal in the book of Romans, immediately following Paul's precise explanation of the good news of God's mercy. This was the message that he had been risking his life to proclaim all over the Roman empire. Mercy means that we haven't received what we ought to have. If I feel mistreated by a shop assistant, it doesn't take long before I say something like "You can't treat me like this, I deserve better. I know my rights . . ." But when I get stopped by the police going through an amber light, I don't want to receive what I deserve. I plead for mercy. In the preceding chapters of Romans, Paul has deliberately explained the consequences of our disobedience to God and the magnitude of our sin to help us realise how close we have come not just to death, but eternal death and punishment. God does not crush us with the full extent of the law for failing his perfect standards, but has forgiven us because of Christ's work on the cross on our behalf. Paul tells us to live our lives in the light of this mercy.

God mercifully grants each new day as a gift to be celebrated. This is true whatever our circumstances and however we feel in the mornings. Many of us feel unable to face the day because of tiredness or sickness, family or work problems, because of the empty space in the bed next to us, or the picture on our bedside table reminding us of a missing part in our lives. David shows us that we can be honest with God about the pain we are experiencing and still express worship. We are not called to wear a fake smile and to pretend all is right with the world. Nevertheless, whatever we face each day, as believers we all have something to be grateful for: God saved us in his mercy. Like David, we can be wide awake to the realities of life in a broken world, yet not be consumed by circumstances. The challenge is for us to start each day by recognising God's merciful sustenance. It only takes a moment, but it affects our attitude to the whole day ahead.

Saving Private Ryan is an epic film about the D-Day landings in Normandy. A squad of soldiers is sent to track down one man. His three brothers had all been killed in battle within days of each other. The mission means that most of the men sent to extract Ryan from the front line will lose their lives. After much bloodshed, with his dying breath the squad's commanding officer whispers to Ryan that he must earn this sacrifice. The film then jumps forward fifty years to a gray-haired old man kneeling next to the war grave of the commander. With tears in his eyes, Ryan recounts that every single day he had remembered the sacrifice paid for him. Ryan realised what his life had cost and he had an appropriate and overwhelming sense of gratitude at being given a second shot at life.

The Bible is clear that we can never earn the forgiveness of God. Our great God planned a rescue mission in which his appropriate judgment on our sin could be poured out on the willing sacrifice of his Son. We can now live in the light of this through the power of the Holy Spirit. We have been given a second shot at life. We've been snatched from the jaws of death, saved from the brink of Hell. Our commanding officer and rescuer, Jesus Christ, does not order us to earn what he has done but asks us to live up to the calling that we have received, by offering ourselves in grateful worship.

Waking up and God's compassion

David's challenging example of waking up in the midst of adversity, yet with worship on his lips, is not unique in the Bible. At first sight the book of Lamentations is depressing. For most of us, the title is discouraging enough to put us off from reading it. The book is indeed a pain-filled cry to God after severe suffering. It consists of five poems of mourning over the devastation caused by God's anger coming on the nation of Israel and its prized capital city, Jerusalem, which has fallen to invaders. The first poem describes the riches-to-rags transformation that the city has undergone: once a queen among cities, now Jerusalem is a slave (1:1). The second poem makes it very clear that this is no accident of history – this is the judgment of God. It is the Lord that has torn down the city (2:1-3). The last two poems are no more encouraging – one outlines the sufferings of Jerusalem under siege and the last is a prayer for mercy. But the third poem, in the center of this most bleak of books, contains a glimmer of hope. The tone becomes personal and Jeremiah the prophet writes in the first person

> I remember my affliction and my wandering, the bitterness and the gall.
> I well remember them, and my soul is downcast within me.
> Yet this I call to mind and therefore I have hope:
> Because of the LORD's great love we are not consumed, for his compassions never fail.
> They are new every morning; great is your faithfulness.
> I say to myself, "The LORD is my portion; therefore I will wait for him."
>
> Lamentations 3:19-24

Like King David who wrote hundreds of years earlier, Jeremiah is mindful of the reality of the pain that he has experienced. But he deliberately chooses to call to mind another fact. God's great love is as much a reality to him as the suffering he is experiencing. The suffering does not overwhelm him, because God's compassion can be relied upon. It is this compassion that Jeremiah declares is new every morning.

For the first readers of Lamentations, this declaration would have reminded them of God's faithfulness to his rebellious people wandering in the desert after being rescued from the slavery of the Egyptians, hundreds of years earlier. Despite their waywardness, he sustained them in the desert. Every morning they received fresh food as a tangible sign of his compassion on them. Despite being in the middle of a wilderness, God showed that he knew where they were and daily provided for their needs. Jeremiah alludes to God's past faithfulness and kindness to inspire hope to keep on trusting God each day despite the circumstances.

As we stretch out in the morning, sometimes the trouble we are going to face in the day ahead seems insurmountable. We feel it would be better if we could just roll over and go back to sleep and hope it will all go away. Jeremiah, writing his lament for the lost glories of his hometown – probably in a cave hiding from the marauding invaders – inspires us. He calls us to face the harsh realities of life, in fact to tell God about the pain we feel and the circumstances we are in, but also to hold on to the precious truth that each day is a new opportunity to experience God's compassion.

Some mornings we wake up and feel short-changed. We could have done with a few more hours of sleep. We may get up and walk around but we are barely conscious. Neither splashing cold water on our faces, nor slapping our cheeks, or even swallowing a triple shot of expresso seem to break the fog out of our heads. When life is hectic, lack of sleep can give daily life the eerie kind of fuzziness that makes us feel like we are walking zombies. But worse than this physical fuzziness is the spiritual fog that we can wake up with. We can get up and start the day, barely conscious of God and his presence in our lives.

Jeremiah's experience of suffering brought him to his senses. Sometimes it is in the hardest times in our lives that God is able to wake us up to the true realities of the world. For those of us who are not currently facing the burden of personal difficulties, the tragedy of life can break through to us through an article on the breakfast news or in the morning paper. As we are roused to do something, or pray something, we are hearing God's wake-up call. As we feel for the world the way that God feels about it, we become wide awake, connecting with God.

[handwritten: God's call is us to worship him with everything]

Waking up and God's call

[handwritten: helps you to think of what Gods heart would be]

Jeremiah and David both begin the day in worship of God. This is not the sort of worship that shuts out the problems around us, but worship that brings God's perspective and character to bear on those problems. Their worship recognised God's mercy and grace, compassion and sovereignty.

[handwritten left margin: spiritual perspective - Gods will exam results n his hands not the end of the world]

If we follow their example and begin the day reflecting on God's unfailing love, we not only set our life in spiritual perspective, we recognise that our life is a gift from God. As we offer up our thanks, we are offering up our worship. This provides us not only with the right perspective on the day ahead, but also with a model for the day ahead. If we worship God in the first moments of our day, we are on our way to worshipping him with every second.

In preparation for speaking at a wedding I watched a show called *Weddings from Hell 3*. Apparently by popular demand, they bring this show out every year. The story was told of a fairytale wedding. The service had gone smoothly, the rings had been remembered, the vicar had got all the lines right and all was looking fine. However, within half an hour of arriving at the reception, the bride disappeared. She had nipped into town to the music store, where the pop singer Ronan Keating was signing his CDs. As she stood in the queue in her beautiful dress, no one could believe it. Even Ronan looked a bit bewildered. And the poor husband who had lost his wife to another man so early on his marriage felt betrayed and disappointed.

Traditionally the church, the bride of Christ, has taught us to attend Sunday morning worship services and have occasional quiet times. Both of these are good in and of themselves but if our worship stops there, God has every right to feel left at the altar, betrayed by his betrothed. God deserves the best of every second: a couple of hours a week is second best.

I am not saying that we should be singing worship songs twenty-four hours a day. Simply getting up with the intention of offering our bodies and the day ahead to God is an act of worship. We can worship God in the middle of every activity, just as we can worship God through our circumstances. As we saw in Romans 12, Paul defines our spiritual worship as an offering of our physical bodies in sacrifice. Most of us have a disembodied, airy-fairy view of spirituality that is difficult to pin down. In stark contrast, Paul's definition of spirituality combines what we do with our bodies and our worshipful relationship with God.

This understanding of spirituality is radical for the church today. It brings worship out of our church buildings and onto our streets. It brings worship out of our quiet times and into our day-to-day living. The spiritual is not simply confined to singing or praying in church, but it is integral to our whole life, even to those physical activities such as eating, drinking, playing sport or getting in and out of bed. Unfortunately our language does not help us remember this fact. We often talk on a Sunday about "a time of worship" or a "worship service." Both of these are good but worship and service need to spill out into every area of our lives and into the community.

Jesus taught and lived a physical spirituality for the sake of others. John's gospel tells us: "The Word became flesh and lived among us." Jesus did not say to the hungry "Go off and find a supermarket." Jesus did not say to the lepers "I can heal your spirit." Jesus touched them physically and he healed them physically. Spiritual and physical belong together, which is why Paul tells us that whatever we do physically, we should do as a spiritual act of worship to God.

This applies to how we wake up in the mornings and everything we do throughout the day. Our attitude and our actions can reflect a lifestyle of sacrificial worship. When we take our bodies out of bed in the morning in honor of God, it is part of our spiritual worship. When we wash and feed ourselves in honor of God, it is part of our spiritual worship.

When we think back to the Garden of Eden, we observe that there was no temple and no church. There was no command to have a quiet time. There was not even a Bible, hymnbooks or the Book of Common Prayer. There were no musicians and no data-projected song words. But God said that the world he created was good, and he commanded Adam and Eve to look after it. As they enjoyed creation, lived in practical obedience and in favor and conversation with God, they honoured him. Their whole life was worship – from the second they awoke in the morning. We need to recapture this holistic approach to worship.

Similarly, the book of Revelation describes the future and tells us that there will be no temple and no church buildings. God's presence will be with us everywhere: the whole of our lives will be lived out in God's company.

This idea of living in God's presence is not confined to the Garden of Eden and Heaven. Because of God's Spirit in us, we are able to enjoy God's presence around the clock. This means that we are living spiritually twenty-four hours a day, whatever we are doing. Imagine a man who says he is only married at home, everywhere else he is single. This is ridiculous. We are not only Christians at church, but everywhere else too – at home, at work, at the supermarket, under the duvet, in the shower. Once we disentangle ourselves from the trap of thinking that worship is only for Sundays and quiet times, we are freed to discover what worship looks like in practice in the everyday activities of our lives.

I almost think this is more important than having a quiet time

Waking up and God's pleasure

Did you know that statistics show that most car accidents happen close to home? I always get more nervous on a long journey than on a quick nip to the shops. But apparently, when people are driving and they are getting closer to home, they switch into autopilot and don't take as much care as they should. That's when accidents happen. We are often on autopilot in our lives, especially in the morning. Shower, dress, hair and make-up, cereal and go. And the problem with autopilot is accidents can happen. We accidentally get stuck in a rut and end up doing things not because they honor God but because that's the way we have always done things.

Isaac Newton woke up one day in the seventeenth century and saw an apple falling off a tree and formulated the law of gravitation. He was not the first person to see an apple falling off a tree. If he were on autopilot, he would have just picked up that famous apple and eaten it. Isaac Newton looked at the apple falling off the tree and thought: "That's odd."

What about Archimedes? He woke up one morning, jumped into the bath, noticed the water level rise, thought "That's odd" and shouted "Eureka." How many people had jumped into baths before Archimedes and never noticed displacement theory? How many times had Archimedes jumped into the bath before that occasion? Yet one morning, something was different.

When we begin the day recognising who God is, this inevitably has an impact on what happens next. We are not on auto-pilot. Whether it is putting sugar on our cereal or watching breakfast TV, we see things from a new perspective and this opens up the possibility of recognising that Christians are called to bring God pleasure by living radically different lives. Paul explores this through a powerful metaphor in his letter to the Ephesians.

> For you were once darkness, but now you are light in the Lord. Live as children of light (for the fruit of the light consists in all goodness, righteousness and truth) and find out what pleases the Lord. Have nothing to do with the fruitless deeds of darkness, but rather expose them. For it is shameful even to mention what the disobedient do in secret. But everything exposed by the light becomes visible, for it is light that makes everything visible. This is why it is said "Wake up, O sleeper, rise from the dead, and Christ will shine on you" (Eph. 5:8-14).

I used to live in a country where power cuts were a regular occurrence. I would come home from work only to find that the entire house was plunged into pitch darkness. As the lights went out, so did hopes of catching a movie, reading a book, or cooking dinner. Often it meant an early night because our supply of candles had run out. When the morning came, the light burst into the house, offering the hope of a new day full of possibilities. But the light also showed up the true state of the house: unwashed dishes, piles of ironing, memos by the phone. Everything the darkness had hidden was now exposed. Paul parallels this with the Christian life. He calls us to live as children of light, which not only brings hope but also exposes the mess we are in. He quotes from an ancient Christian service, probably from a baptism or Easter: "Wake o sleeper, rise from the dead and Christ will shine on you." Becoming a Christian is like being roused from a coma and means allowing the light of the risen Son to shine in our lives. Every new morning is a new opportunity to see our lives as they really are and, with God's help, live lives that will please him.

Oliver Stone directed *JFK*, a fascinating film about the assassination of US President John F. Kennedy in 1967. The film is told from the perspective of the district attorney who was supposed to oversee the case. The film describes a massive cover-up. The attorney has to make a choice. Will he look the other way and go with the official story and enjoy a trouble-free life? Or will he put his career, livelihood and family on the line and follow through with the truth that he knows? In the middle of this moral dilemma, his wife calls him to bed, as it is getting late. The attorney says: "I am wide-awake, in fact I am more awake than I have ever been in my life. I can't go to sleep now ..."

The call to follow Christ is to be truly awake, to see the whole of life in the light of the truth of God's Son. This book begins with this invitation to become fully awake to the possibilities of life spent in the light. We need to be roused from sleepwalking through life on autopilot, and instead live deliberately and passionately for God, both enjoying his blessings and seeking to please him. In this way we worship God twenty-four hours of the day. For those of us who look back on our life and see how we have failed to do this in the past, we can be encouraged that one great thing about waking up is that it symbolises a fresh start. As Christians, we understand that we need that again and again. In God's mercy, whatever we might have failed to do yesterday, we have a chance to do today.

Waking up in the morning is more than getting out of bed. From David, we see that waking up is a gift of God's mercy. From Jeremiah we see that facing the day ahead is an opportunity to experience God's faithfulness and compassion. From Paul we learn that each new morning is a rousing challenge to live intentionally for God in the light of his mercy. God's wake-up call to each of us is to enjoy life in the Spirit in every aspect of our physical life, and to please him in each day ahead.

Just a minute

What we do with our bodies can and must be a spiritual act of worship to God. When your alarm goes off, remember it is a timely reminder not only to get out of bed, but also to offer up your day to God, whatever the circumstances. As you switch on your bedside light, remember to live your day in the light of God's mercy. Switch on your light, and switch off the autopilot, consciously talking to God as you wash and dress, thanking him for all he has given you, and asking him to show you how you can use your physical being in worship today. Praise God for his world as you open the curtains. Offer God the day ahead.

Thank God for the relationships he has given you as you meet the other members of your household in the morning. Take time to ask them how they are feeling about the day ahead. As you turn off the security system or unlock the front door, remind yourself who is the stronghold of your life. As you pick up the paper or the post, pray for those people whose lives are represented in your hands. As you turn on the news, pray for the suffering world in which we live. As you feed the cat or let out the dog, remind yourself of the Person who is taking care of all your everyday needs. When you are pouring out your cup of tea, ask God how you can pour yourself out in a spiritual act of worship to him that day.

John 4 v 23-24
"Its who you are + the way you live that count before God. Your worship must engage your spirit in the pursuit of truth. Thats the kind of people the father is looking out for: those who are simply + honestly themselves before him in worship. God is sheer being itself — spirit. Those their who worship must do it

On your iPod

Wake Up, Boo Radleys, (Sony Music, 1995)
Bring Me To Life, Evanescence (Epic, 2004)
Let Everything That Has Breath, Matt Redman (Kingsway, 1997)
Holy, Holy, Holy, Lord God Almighty, Reginald Heber (1896)
I Say A Little Prayer For You, Aretha Franklin (Atlantic Records, 1968)

Off the shelf

Robert Banks, *Redeeming the Routines* (Grand Rapids: Baker Academic, 2001)
Thomas Watson, *The Godly Man's Picture* (London: Banner of Truth, 1998)
Duncan Banks, *Breakfast with God: Spiritual Food for Every Day* (Grand Rapids: Zondervan, 2002)
Ruth Valerio, *L Is For Lifestyle* (Leicester: IVP, 2004)
Alister McGrath, *Beyond the Quiet Time* (London: Triangle, 1995)

out of their every being, their spirits their true selves in adoration. "

COMMUTE

DRIVING UNDER THE INFLUENCE

Drive me crazy

Something very strange happened recently. When I went on a day out with some friends, I noticed that people I knew as polite, mild mannered, businesslike individuals got into a car, drove a few miles down the road, entered a shed and came out mean, rowdy, rough and ready for battle. What a transformation, and all in the name of paint-balling. The people that went into the shed were mechanics, accountants, students and cabin crew. The people that came out were commandos, mercenaries, soldiers of fortune and psychopaths.

This is not such an uncommon sight. A son leaves the house and heads for the bus. When he reaches his stop, he is no longer a son, but a businessman: smart, respectable and ready to cut to the quick with a hot deal. Or a mother drops the kids off at the childminders, and gets back into the car, only to emerge half an hour later as a legal expert, with a queue of clients demanding her time. What has happened to these people? They are thrust from one world into another. Home is far behind them. The transportation has become a vehicle of transformation. It doesn't matter if the journey was two minutes or two hours: in the time it takes for them to commute to work, worlds have been swapped.

In fact the word commute means "swap". If a prison sentence is commuted, it has been changed from one form to another. So when we commute, we swap the world of sofas, parent-teacher meetings and home cooked meals to swivel chairs, board meetings and fast food.

In Bible times, this distinction between work and home just did not exist for most people. With cottage industries such as farming or carpentry, most people worked from home and had one identity. Twenty-first century work/home distinction is a relatively new concept, and brings about two separate spheres of existence with different expectations, routines and social networks in each world, two identities separated by a journey.

Paradoxically, the advent of broadband, Blackberries and bluetooth allow the two identities to overlap. We can take our work home. With a ring on the phone, we can commute from family to work mode over the dinner table or at the local pub. In this situation, it is very hard to remember who we are supposed to be where. Identity is an issue that is up for debate. As we constantly swap between worlds, do we ever stop to think what effect this may be having on us and our worship?

Prepare for take-off

When some friends of mine went on a hiking holiday to Peru, they stopped over briefly in Lima, a city at sea level. They then took their connecting flight into the 15,000-foot high mountains to pick up the Inca trail. During this short flight from low to high altitude, they experienced pressure sickness: headaches and nausea. One of them even passed out. Divers have a similar experience if they surface from a deep-sea dive too quickly. We too can get the bends when surfacing too quickly from home or work. Like the diver, we need a decompression chamber to help us prepare for the transition from one world to another. This is not a bad image for our commute. We can learn to see the journey itself not as an extra pressure, but as a God-given opportun-ity to depressurise and reorientate.

Nor do we need to limit the scope of this to journeys to work. As we leave home to visit our sick relatives, as we go from household routine to family holiday, as we criss-cross the country going to weddings, parties and funerals, as we walk round the corner to the shops, take the bus to church or visit the neighbor next door, we are all involved in journeys between very different worlds, each with its own pressures. However far we go, however long it takes, we all journey during the week, we all swap worlds.

The first time I traveled by airplane without my parents I was sixteen, I was a new Christian, I was responsible for my thirteen-year-old sister and I was on a long-haul flight to Malaysia. I was extremely nervous and I felt very alone. As we reached cruise altitude the dawn sun was setting the sky ablaze with color, in a way that is always so much more vibrant when you are above the clouds. It was one of those moments where God spoke to me perfectly through his Word. I flipped open my Bible and read

> Where can I go from your Spirit?
> Where can I flee from your presence?
> If I go up to the heavens, you are there;
> if I make my bed in the depths, you are there.
> If I rise on the wings of the dawn,
> if I settle on the far side of the sea,
> even there your hand will guide me,
> your right hand will hold me fast
>
> (Ps. 139:7-10).

At 35,000 feet, I realised that God was with me and he would be with me when I landed. There was nowhere on the planet where I would be separated from him.

Wherever our journeys take us, whatever situations we face when we travel to work, to hospital appointments or home, our God is with us. What a privilege to know that God's presence is as real in our office as it is in our worship services. The commute gives us time to acquaint ourselves with the presence of God that doesn't change, no matter where we end up.

This fact was underlined to the prophet Ezekiel 2,600 years ago. He had been forcibly relocated to a land far away from his home and his future dreams of being a priest in

God's temple were shattered, as he became first a refugee and then a slave. But God wanted Ezekiel and all the captured Israelites to know that he had not abandoned them. So he gave Ezekiel a vision

As I looked at the living creatures, I saw a wheel on the ground beside each creature with its four faces. This was the appearance and structure of the wheels: They sparkled like chrysolite, and all four looked alike. Each appeared to be made like a wheel intersecting a wheel. As they moved, they would go in any one of the four directions the creatures faced; the wheels did not turn about as the creatures went. Their rims were high and awesome, and all four rims were full of eyes all around.

When the living creatures moved, the wheels beside them moved; and when the living creatures rose from the ground, the wheels also rose. Wherever the spirit would go, they would go, and the wheels would rise along with them, because the spirit of the living creatures was in the wheels. When the creatures moved, they also moved; when the creatures stood still, they also stood still; and when the creatures rose from the ground, the wheels rose along with them, because the spirit of the living creatures was in the wheels (Ezek. 1:15-21).

God's vision to Ezekiel of his throne with whirring wheels moving in every direction re-emphasised his presence to his exiled people in Babylon. He would be with his people in exile just as he had been with them in the Promised Land. God's reign has no borders or boundaries. God rules wherever his people roam.

Our time in a car or on a train between worlds can be seen as God-given. Often traffic jams, train delays, turbulence, standing room only and road rage envelope us with anxiety and stress. But as we see this time as a decompression chamber as opposed to another of life's pressures, we will more readily be able to maintain a godly perspective on our different worlds. The Bible encourages us time and again to cast our burdens onto God, not to be anxious about anything –

but to pray. As we worry about what we have left behind, or the situation we are about to walk into, we can let our commute be an opportunity to pray and enjoy our relationship with the Creator of the Universe, for whom no problem is too big or too small, and who journeys with us wherever we go.

A journal of a journey

In the last chapter we saw how our physical life can be spiritual worship to God. If this is true how best can we appreciate and make the most of the time that we spend traveling? How can the journey itself be worship to God? Is our life on auto-pilot, or cruise control, or do we have our God at the helm?

We need to see first of all that the Bible is a journal of a journey. All the smaller trips we make in our daily routine can be understood firstly in light of the ultimate journey. Even our voyage from cradle to grave must be seen within the whole sweep of human history, a journey that begins in a garden and ends in a city.

I like to watch how friends prepare for the arrival of a new baby. Some prepare well in advance and have the furniture, clothes, toys and nursery school place almost from conception. Others are more laid back, still painting walls as contractions intensify. Somehow or other, they all get there in the end, and the newborn is brought back from the hospital into a suitable and beautiful place – their first home.

The first two chapters of Genesis describe God preparing a place to bring new life. Instead of a mobile, he hung the stars in place. Instead of toys in drawers, God hid gold underground for us to find. Instead of wallpaper, friezes and easy-peel transfers, God created mountains, seas, trees and flowers. Nobody could doubt God's love for the life he was bringing into the world. He was not expecting human beings just to exist, but to thrive and prosper, explore and develop and enjoy themselves.

Compare God's creation of earth to our images of heaven. We often picture not a physical place but an abstract wispy expectation of clouds, angels and expansion of space. Our imagination is severely limited. Not so God's. When he created the world, he made a place for us: a wonderfully diverse and tangible place. God made us physical and spiritual beings and put us in a physical place that he affirmed was good: the Garden of Eden.

When our children do something wrong, we might punish them by banishing them from the scene of the crime, from our company and, most importantly, from their beloved toys. Unfortunately the same thing happened to the human race. We showed that we were not to be trusted in the wonderful garden God created for us. When he banished us from Eden, God set angels to guard the doors, and the journey of history began.

In our spirit, we know that we are in a "time out" and we long to be back in the place God made for us. The next stage of the Bible story sees Cain wandering the earth and Abraham and Moses journeying to find the Promised Land. Even there, God's people rebel and need to be banished to exile in Babylon. As they trickle back over the centuries, God eventually sends Jesus to earth. Because of what Jesus accomplished on the cross, we are no longer exiles. We are in God's presence wherever we are because of his Spirit living in us. However this time, instead of gathering us together, he scatters us all over the world with a mission. We are to be aliens and strangers in the world, living by faith in God despite opposition.

All through this amazing story of amazing people and amazing journeys, there is a longing. There is a homesickness that resonates within each of us that we are not yet truly at home. We are driven by this homesickness which is

[handwritten left margin: wherever we are not just in godly places.]

[handwritten: I do plan on doing this am I too comfortable with where I am]

[handwritten bottom: am I really living by faith?]

for a place that we have never seen or been to, a longing for heaven, where God is preparing a place for us (John 14:1-3). In the book of Revelation God uses the image of a city to describe the end of the journey: heaven. For a persecuted church the picture of a city would have been a powerful one, reminding them that though they were <u>nobodies at the mercy of the authorities,</u> one day they would be the <u>honored citizens of a mighty metropolis.</u> The city is also a picture of c<u>ommunity</u> and for a minority group who had come to depend on one another, the idea that their relationships would not just be with God but with their fellow travelers must have encouraged them greatly. How different is this description to the ethereal clouds in the sky that we were noting before. God has made us physical and spiritual and we are reminded that we must consider the two together, which <u>elevates our everyday mundane lives into God-given opportunities to worship in spirit and truth.</u>

Now that we have taken our bearings using the major landmarks of the journey of human history, we can also learn from the Bible how we should travel our leg of the journey. What the Bible offers are trailblazers: people who have traveled ahead of us and who can show us the way.

> By faith Abraham, when called to go to a place he would later receive as his inheritance, <u>obeyed and went, even though he did not know where he was going.</u> By faith he made his home in the promised land like a stranger in a foreign country; he lived in tents, as did Isaac and Jacob, who were heirs with him of the same promise. For he was <u>looking forward to the city with foundations, whose architect and builder is God</u> (Heb. 11:8-10).

Which way now?

I was broken down in the first lane of Albania's only dual carriageway. The bonnet of the wreck of an Alfa Romeo I was in

---

[Handwritten notes in top margin:] John 14 v1-4. Don't let this throw you. You trust God don't you? Trust me. there is plenty of room for you in my fathers home. If that weren't so, would I have told you that I'm on my way to get a room ready for you? And if I'm on my way to get a room

[Handwritten notes in right margin:] I'll come back + get you so you can live where I live. And you already knew the road I'm taking / live in the same tent as God.

[Handwritten notes in left margin:] God is / in the wrong place and up / Even if you end up in the wrong place God is

was open in front of me. My plane was going to depart in twenty minutes, and I was thirty-five minutes away from the airport traveling at a legal speed. Agron, my Albanian neighbor's cousin, was fiddling with the petrol tank: a plastic cola bottle. Fuel was leaking everywhere and the lit cigarette in his mouth was making me nervous. It was one of those times when I wondered how exactly I had got myself into this position and where I was going to end up.

Many Christians are drifters. The degrees we study, the jobs we choose, the spouses we end up with, and the places we retire to are often down to the path of least resistance. But that is not the way that God intended life to be. The book of Hebrews was written to avoid drift (Heb. 2:1). The writer is warning a group of Jewish believers about the danger of drifting away from God, slipping back to the supposed security of Judaism. Hebrews 11 offers an alternative approach to faith by inspiring its readers with examples of people who refused to go with the flow. In pride of place in this chapter stands Abraham, the hero to whom most of the verses are devoted. When we travel we must not be like those Jews drifting through life, and drifting away from God. We must be like Abraham sent on a journey by God.

I am sure Abraham had to ask himself many times where he was going. He couldn't answer this question geographically, as God had not given him a satellite navigation system with a postcode destination finder and precise voice prompts at every junction. Abraham's answer was not geographical but theological. His future location could only be explained by his current vocation. Abraham's life was set in motion by responding to God's call and his direction was decided by God himself.

Could we answer the question "Where are we going?" with the same theological insight? A postcode or precise latitude and longitude are not adequate answers for Christians when trying to answer the question of our location.

Its crucial we keep a firm grip on what we've heard so that we don't drift off.

Perhaps we are switched off to God's call on our life. After all, what if God was to call us to go somewhere we do not want to go? We have our usual excuses: I am too old – so was Abraham. I have family here – so had Abraham. I want to start a family – so did Abraham.

It often happens that when young people leave home and go to University, they seem to lose their faith. And of course there are plenty of distractions when they are away from home for the first time. But it begs the question – back home – <u>were they actually trusting God, or were they trusting their location?</u> It's easy to sit and judge from the confines of the lounges we have sat in for the past ten years. It is not only young people who trust their location. Would our faith crumble too if we were uprooted from the safe environment we are in at the moment?

God could ask us to "Go" at any time, and the correct response is not necessarily "Where to?" but "<u>Which way?</u>" Abraham did not know his final destination but he was given directions along the way. He is a hard act to follow. God called Abraham away from Ur, but did not tell him where he was going. <u>God called him away from security and wealth into trouble, famine and hardship.</u> Abraham was willing to let God into the driving seat of his life. He was prepared to travel in the opposite direction to where common-sense would have sent him, in order to prove his total allegiance to God.

When we next get into our cars, or onto a train, plane, bus or bike, we can ask ourselves whether our journeys are headed in the right direction.

Travel in style

When we first meet Abraham he is a rich and important businessman, an upstanding member of his family and

who cares if people say its dangerous or what about money or wouldn't you rather study or get a job first just do what God wants community. But when God changed the direction of his life, he also changed his status. Abraham became a refugee, a stranger in a strange land. His family home became a tent and he did not even speak the same language as his new neighbors.

God calls us to become refugees too. Peter tells us that we are to consider ourselves "aliens and strangers in the world" (1 Pet. 2:11). When people see us, they need to notice that we do not belong, not because of the way we look or speak but because of the way we are.

I have stayed in a wide variety of hotels. Some were spacious, spotless and spectacular. I have also stayed in the other kind – hotels with damp sheets and stinking drains and creatures moving across the floor. I have seen a lot of rooms with peeling wallpaper, thin unattractive curtains and broken appliances. However, I don't usually travel with my tool kit, Ikea catalogue and pot of paint. Because I am passing through, there is no need to get settled. Abraham did not need to dig foundations and start building himself a house; he knew he was passing through and needed to be ready to move on to obey God's call on his life to serve the nations. Similarly, we too should have the attitude that we are "only passing through" on our journey, with the same purpose as Abraham; that of serving the nations.

We often expect to travel through life in style. Our cars are new, our train seats are reserved, and we may even upgrade to first class occasionally. We complain at traffic jams and train delays, as though they ought not happen to us. It is hard to be a refugee – they never travel first class. They stow away in the cargo hold of trucks, hop onto the backs of trains and get deported by planes in handcuffs. The way we travel through life is as important as the direction in which we are going. Abraham as our lead vehicle shows that we need to travel light, and show people the light of God as we travel. Of course Abraham is only a pale shadow of Jesus himself. Jesus too was a refugee. Jesus also was homeless. Jesus traveled from place to place. Jesus faced all manner of difficulties. Yet Jesus was the true light of the world.

As people of faith, we need to emulate Abraham and Jesus. However we may be put off when we read what happens to people of faith in Hebrews 11, "others were tortured and refused to be released ... some faced jeers and flogging ... while others were chained and put in prison. They were stoned; they were sawn in two; they were put to death by the sword. They went about in sheepskins and goatskins, destitute, persecuted and ill treated ..." There are no red carpets for Christians in this world. This leg of our journey is not going to be an easy ride, in fact wherever we go we are promised persecution. *at work* ↑*it will be the same in this country as in a foreign one.*

The Bible teaches us that as we travel around we can depressurize by lifting our burdens onto the Lord who carries them for us. We should regularly check our direction to see that it is in line with God's call on our lives. We should also check if we are really living as strangers in the world. Of course, not so strange that we do not engage with the people around us as Jesus did, getting alongside them, involved in their lives and demonstrating God's compassion. But strange enough to be distinguishable from the people that belong to this world, not drifting and conforming to their pattern of life.

Are we prepared to make sacrifices as we travel like Abraham did? Are we willing to close our laptops to befriend the person sitting next to us? Are we prepared to change our fuel or mode of transport to reduce our carbon footprint? Are we polite and gracious to other road users? Sacrifices like these will remind us that we are not traveling in style, and enable us to avoid drift, shining out to the world.

Arrive

I am very familiar with the Piccadilly Line, heading from central London to north-west London. On this journey something very strange happens just past Acton. The first time I took this train I noticed that people around me begin to swear, first quietly under their breath, and then in a more and more agitated way. As I wondered what was going on I realised that we were no longer headed towards Heathrow Airport but towards Uxbridge. I started to check my watch anxiously in fear of missing my flight. What I should have done was to check where the train was headed before boarding. It always says on the front of the train, so there was no excuse.

Most people are like that with life. We forget to check where we are headed. We just sit comfortably until it is too late. Abraham did not know where he was going, but he did trust the person he was following. We have the enormous benefit of knowing exactly who we are following and where it is we are going. For the Christian, the destination is all-important. The longing that we talked about earlier, that God put in human hearts since we were thrown out of paradise, is a homing beacon to draw us to the heavenly city.

A friend of mine approaching her wedding day was in utter confusion. Her husband-to-be had promised her an amazing honeymoon – but it was to be a surprise. "All you need is your passport" he had told her. The problem with this was that she had no idea what to pack. Were they headed for a beach holiday in Tahiti, a snowboarding holiday in Canada, or a city break in Paris? Did she need suntan lotion or ski-gear? Did she need vaccinations or visas? How could she possibly prepare?

For our final destination, we do not need to pack anything. Death even does away with our bodies. When we get to heaven we will be provided with new bodies and all that we need. If we consider life to be a journey to that city, then the accumulation of earthly possessions is not part of our preparation for heaven. Yet we still do need to prepare. We need to exchange our money for a new currency and we need to start to practice the customs and skills needed in our new culture. As we learn to worship God through interaction with other people and the world around us, we are learning the language of heaven. As we become more Christ-like in this life we are being acclimatized for our future.

Abraham was preparing to go to a city with foundations, another way God used to describe Zion, his city. These foundations contrasted with the tent pegs that had previously held down his home. The wonderful promise of the destination enabled Abraham to put up with the temporary discomforts of nomadic life. Abraham's future was certain so he didn't need to worry about security in the here and now. In the same way God has promised and secured us a bright future, so we can put up with the difficulties, persecutions and discomforts of our present living.

Some people talk about being too heavenly minded to be any earthly good. However, Hebrews argues that we need to be heavenly minded in order to be any earthly good. By keeping our destination in mind, we can live correctly in the here and now.

Drive

We can experience God in the commute by seeing our journeys in the light of God's bigger journey described for us on the pages of the Bible. We can also experience God in the commute by remembering God's presence is with us wherever we go and by asking him to transform and redeem it into useful decompression time. In our departure, our direction, our destitution and our destination, we should keep focussed until we finally arrive home, in heaven with God. The drive of our life is to be worship to God, recognising him at the steering wheel of our lives wherever we go and allowing him to set the direction and the pace.

Whatever transportation we use, whatever transformation we go through; son to businessman, mother to legal expert, mild-mannered men into Rambo look-alikes, there is one final truth to remember. Wherever we go, whoever we have to be, we do not change our primary identity. We are first and foremost children of God. In our transformations in the name of work or family or responsibility, God also remains the same. He has never changed throughout history, the Alpha and Omega, the Beginning and End, and yet the same yesterday, today and forever.

Just a minute

Before you leave on a journey ask God for his presence with you. As you check the map, check that you are headed in the right direction by reviewing where your life is going. As you find your seat, check your attitude remembering you are not yet first-class passengers but aliens and strangers. As you type in your destination on your SatNav, or check the departures board, remind yourself that you are really on your way to heaven.

Inspire your commute by placing some landmarks on your journey. Whether you walk, drive or take public transport, whenever you pass a school, pray for the next generation; when you pass a police station, pray for justice in the world. Occasionally take a different route to remind yourself not to live life on auto-pilot.

Unless you are driving, take your Bible, a novel or a newspaper to read on the journey and ask God to speak through the pages to get you up to speed with your interaction with the world. Read a book about work on the way to work and a book about family on the way home to help your transformation process. Listen to sermons or worship songs to help you focus your mind on God. (But please keep your hands on the steering wheel!)

Look around at the other people when you are commuting. They are in the same decompression chamber as you, but most of them are not prepared for their final destination. Pray for them, reach out to them, befriend them and help them as you travel. Look around at the world when you are commuting. Thank God for the wonderful place that he prepared for you. Think about any changes you need to make to your mode of transport to protect the world you live in. Pray for the different towns and countries you travel through. Keep a journal of your journeys. A friend used to put a Bible verse next to the speedometer to keep his velocity in check. I know of others who donate their air miles to charity or to Christian missionaries.

These are all suggestions of how we can worship God as we travel. As we integrate some of these ideas into our lives, we are practising 24-hour faith and worship.

On the iPod

Drive, The Cars (Elektra Records, 1984)
Buck Rogers, Feeder (The Echo Label, 2001)
Homeward Bound, Simon and Garfunkel (Colombia Records, 1965)
To Be A Pilgrim, John Bunyan (1684)
Blessed Be Your Name, Beth & Matt Redman (Kingsway, 2002)

Off the shelf

Alain de Botaine, *The Art of Travel* (London: Penguin, 2003)
Jack Kerouac, *On the Road* (London: Penguin, 2003)
Vincent Donovan, *Christianity Rediscovered* (London: SCM, 2001)
Chua Wee Hian, *Getting Through Customs* (Leicester: IVP, 1992)
Alister McGrath, *The Journey: A Pilgrim In the Lands of the Spirit* (London: Hodder & Stoughton, 1999)

WORK

DOING BUSINESS WITH GOD

Preoccupation with occupation

When I was a church minister, I used to smile inwardly during small talk at parties, as I waited for someone to ask that inevitable question: "So what is it you do?" The question usually came soon after a moan about the weather or the volume of the music. I knew they were asking me because they wanted to size me up and measure me on a scale of social significance, and I knew they would be fazed by my reply. At first there would be no sense of unease: I was inconsequential on the social pecking order and posed no sort of threat to their egos. Then a sort of spiritual unease would emerge. I could see people replaying the small talk in their heads, checking for swear words or other faux pas. Then there would be an awkward silence, at which point I would take pity on them and help them out a bit by asking what they did for a job.

My wife, who has spent a number of years as a full-time mother, also used to dread the question "And what do you do?" For a while she told people she worked from home, making sure she could quickly divert attention by offering a plate of crisps. Full-time mothers and church ministers never gain much respect at these sorts of events because there is a preoccupation with occupation, and we come bottom of the heap.

In order to boost morale, it has become commonplace to provide titles for jobs that an employee could be proud of at a party. A sanitation manager sounds much better than a toilet cleaner. A corporate administrative professional sounds better than a secretary. On these lines, I should have retitled my job "Senior pastoral manager" and introduced my wife as a "Chief domestic officer."

Job titles were even more significant a few hundred years ago. People were even named after their profession. But the Mr Smiths and Mrs Taylors were never replaced in the *Yellow*

Pages by Mr Salesmen and Mrs Technicians, let alone the Ms Corporate Administrative Professional. Whereas previously people could kill two birds with one stone as they introduced themselves, now we have to tell people our name and our profession via two questions. Nevertheless, whether we like it or not, our job defines us in some way, and this has been true throughout history. In fact, someone once said that we should not really be called "human beings" but "human doings", because our identity is so often encapsulated in our chosen profession.

Part of the reason for this blurring of identity and occupation is because work is often the focus of our lives. It begins when we start our education. It takes up the best years of our lives, and the best hours of our days. We work five or six days a week, eleven months of the year for forty or fifty years. The 9 to 5 routine of working life takes up the major proportion of our lives, after sleeping. This leaves hardly any time for anything else – eating, shopping, holidays, family and God. Or does it?

Do we Christians also define ourselves by our job title, or by the significance of our work compared to those around us? Do we measure ourselves against the world's standards of how much money we earn and how much prestige or power our jobs command? Do we feel proud or embarrassed when asked the inevitable dinner party "icebreaker"?

We not only need a far bigger picture of our own identity, we also need a far bigger picture of work if the first calling on our lives is to be full-time worshipping Christians. The Bible provides a description of work which echoes realistically with our own experience of drudgery but also envisions us for understanding God, serving God and worshipping God, redefining terms like boss, ambition, and earning so that we can do business with God, whatever our job.

Handwritten margin notes:

Left margin: provided you/god made us partly to work - he had to - but to bue up such a big place - ten of our lives?

Right margin: we can be — in the work place — we can worship God in the work place — a real obvious witness in the work place

Bottom: How would that go down at a party - im a full time worshipping Christian - I must try it some time - he he

Business plan

Who is the first person mentioned in the Bible as doing any work? It is not Cain, who worked the soil or Noah, builder of the ark, but God himself. In the first chapters of Genesis God is seen to be a designer, builder, gardener, teacher, caretaker, legislator, social worker and tailor. God is at work in the universe. He builds it out of nothing, displaying a sense of order and design and incredible detail. He sustains and maintains his creation, visiting his garden regularly. He teaches human beings how they are to live and then he works to enforce the laws they break. Out of compassion he provides help for them in how to relate to one another and to him, and he provides garments to cover their newly found nakedness.

We see God at work, and as human beings made in God's image we are created to work too. Work is not a part of the fall; it is part of our calling to be like our Creator. Our work provides us with opportunities to understand God, his pleasures and emotions, and with opportunities to demonstrate God's character to a watching universe. God's work also demonstrates that our work is significant. If work is not too lowly an activity for the majestic triune God to participate in – then our work is elevated in importance. As we work, we are like God.

Christian art groups tell us that we worship a creative God and that is where our creativity comes from. This is true: God creates so much diversity in his universe that zoologists can spend a lifetime exploring the animal kingdom and still barely scratch the surface; cosmologists can spend their careers searching the heavens with space-based telescopes and still only observe a tiny fraction of the universe. God's creativity is immense and one of the joys of studying science and working in the arts is to be able to marvel at our heavenly Father's artistry and demonstrate that part of God's nature to the people around us. However, not all of us are naturally creative or scientific, and sometimes we can feel inadequate. But the good news is that God's work is more than that of creation. God sustains the universe, making sure every atom is in its right place, sending the rain (Acts 11) and bringing out the stars (Isa. 40). This sustaining work may not feel as dramatic or exciting as creation, but it is a vital job that God does day in, day out, because of his faithfulness. For those of us in jobs that do not involve a lot of creativity or science, we can relate to God as the Sustainer of the universe, and reflect God's faithful reliability day after day, modeling God's character to the world around us.

Situation vacant

God demonstrates the dignity of work from day one by being the first worker. And God employs human beings from day one (or day six according to Genesis.) We often think of our jobs as the bane of our lives, a regretful obligation to pay off the mortgage, but work was supposed to be an integral aspect of life even before the fall; it was part of the good and unspoilt creation plan.

Some people have used the Bible to try to prove that men should be workers, and women should not work. At first sight, God created Adam and gave him a job to do. But immediately God noted that *in his work*, Adam required a "helper". Not a servant, but a co-worker, a colleague, a companion. And so God created Eve to complement Adam in his work. God created men and women to work together. I am not advocating here that both men and women should necessarily go out and find paid work. In the Genesis account there is no mention of money changing hands, and those of us not in paid employment should not be made to feel second-class. Work is most appropriately understood as the tasks that we do or the responsibilities that we have in the kitchen, in the office, at the factory or in the garden.

Back at the dinner party, when my wife is embarrassed by the question of what she does, she knows that the questioner is wrongly assuming that real work takes place out of the home and involves taxable income. Choosing to work as a houseparent involves coping with social as well as financial pressures. But the Bible does not specify that work has to be paid to be significant, it does not specify which parent (if any) stays at home to look after children: the Bible teaches that we are all called to work and that all work is valued.

In physics we are told that work = mass x distance: the expenditure of energy necessary to do something. God intended work to be us expending energy, whether physical or mental energy, in order to get his job done. God commissioned human beings as his reps, to care for creation on his behalf. Christians are called to work and this means expending our God-given energies serving God, representing him by caring for the creation, caring for and cultivating the planet, and demonstrating God's love to the people he created in his image.

The daily grind

Paul's first letter to the Thessalonians begins with the words. "We continually remember before our God and Father your work produced by faith, your labor prompted by love, and your endurance inspired by hope in the Lord Jesus Christ." It is not surprising that this letter is full of helpful reminders to those of us who find work a labor and something to be endured. Paul talks about success and failure, and about impure motives, flattery and greed. He also reminds them of his own toil and hardship as he worked night and day. He is referring to his two jobs of preaching the gospel and tent-making to earn a living. Paul is keen to sympathise with the Thessalonians' feeling that work is often a slog.

Back at the party, after our job titles are compared and we go on to discuss our differing fields of work, someone is likely to say: "It's not a great job, but it pays the bills." If our jobs do not earn us respect and prestige, at least they earn us our keep. This is not a completely improper view of work. Paul encourages the Thessalonians and us to work to be independent, just as he had set the example. The Bible teaches that we are responsible to earn money if we can, so we can live independently and provide for those who are not able to work and are dependent on us.

"Make it your ambition to lead a quiet life, to mind your own business and to work with your hands, just as we told you, so that your daily life may win the respect of outsiders and so that you will not be dependent on anybody"(1 Thess. 4:11-12). ✳ *don't get depts*

However, these same verses also emphasise that there is something apart from money that needs to be earned by our work. We are to earn, or win the respect of outsiders. There is to be both a financial element and a missionary component to our jobs. As we work, our conduct can be a means through which those that are not yet Christians are helped to see the truth of the gospel lived out in our lives.

Other people at the party make excuses for their chosen profession by prefacing it with the words: "for my sins." Again there is an element of truth in this. Many of our jobs are so tedious they feel like God's punishment on humanity. Our work can be frustrating and difficult.

Work now is not as God originally intended. Before the fall, work was a joy, the office was a garden, our colleagues were perfect in every way, and our boss was God himself. Now our working environment feels less like a garden paradise, and more like a battle zone and there is a good reason for this. When we were banished from the garden because of our inability to respect the boss, there came consequences. These affected every area of our life.

> Cursed is the ground because of you;
> through painful toil you will eat of it
> all the days of your life.
> It will produce thorns and thistles for you,
> and you will eat the plants of the field.
> By the sweat of your brow
> you will eat your food
> until you return to the ground,
> since from it you were taken;
> for dust you are
> and to dust you will return (Gen. 3:17-19).

It is here in Genesis 3 that work mutates into toil. Notice God did not take away work; the intent was still there for it to be a satisfying and integral part of our living, and a means of providing food and nourishment. But it was not going to be totally pleasurable, as it had been; the pleasure was to turn to pain. This curse explains why we often get that sinking feeling on a Monday morning. It is why office life is awkward and we don't always get on with the boss. It is why the stock market goes up and down, and many face bankruptcy or lawsuits. It is why we sometimes feel at the end of our tether. It is why the weeds and the dust are never gone for long. It is why we spend five days of the week longing for Friday night. We eke out our existence in a broken and damaged world, and often it feels like an unending losing battle.

The Greek myth of Sisyphus resonates with many people's experience of work as toil. Zeus punished Sisyphus, and he was cursed to roll a huge stone to the top of a hill and push it down the other side. Sisyphus never completed this task – as soon as he got anywhere close to the top, he was forced back by the sheer weight of the rock, which then pushed him back to the bottom of the hill to start all over again.

In the daily grind of our working lives many of us can relate to Sisyphus. The maintenance men on the Forth Bridge, as soon as they finish one coat of paint, need to start again immediately. Some teachers feel the same – they have just taught thirty children how to read or do multiplication, when a new year starts with thirty fresh faces with no clue. A cleaner scrubs the house from top to bottom only to see the family walk in, wipe their dirty feet and create more washing up and ironing. In fact work often feels like a blunt pencil – pointless.

Employee of the month

So how should we view work, as a blessing or as a curse, as the part of our life we have to endure to enable us to enjoy our time off, or as a gift from God enabling us to be like our Creator? We can get a clue from looking at the life of Jesus.

When John introduces Jesus, he shows people the radical nature of Christianity. Jesus is the Word, who was with God in his work of Creation. This Word became flesh and lived in the physical dimension of planet earth, among us, his own people, blinded to who He was. Jesus is baptised by John, calls his disciples and begins his work, endorsing a wedding celebration, devastating the temple activities, speaking with a Samaritan woman and healing a man who couldn't walk – on the Sabbath. This was a step too far for some people:

> The man went away and told the Jews that it was Jesus who had made him well. So, because Jesus was doing these things on the Sabbath, the Jews persecuted him. Jesus said to them, "My Father is always at his work to this very day, and I, too, am working." For this reason the Jews tried all the harder to kill him; not only was he

Jesus work was anything God wanted him to do + God gives us the power to do exactly the same work as Jesus did-healing + helping the only thing we cant do is die on the cross - the hardest part has been done for us!

breaking the Sabbath, but he was even calling God his own Father, making himself equal with God (John 5:15-18).

As justification for the healing, Jesus called on his relationship with God, his Father, who is always working. This incensed the Jewish leaders – he was breaking the Sabbath and claiming to be equal with God.

Jesus' example teaches us firstly that God is still working. God did not create the world and then go on vacation, leaving us at the mercy of nature. God continues to work and continues to be in control. Secondly, Jesus reveals to us God's work, because his work is the same. Jesus' work was healing the sick or restoring people's self image, like the Samaritan who felt rejected by the Jews, her ex-husbands, and the community around her. Jesus' work was ultimately about bringing salvation to the world through his death in our place. Thirdly, Jesus reveals to us the work we should be doing. If we call God our Father, we should be part of his search and rescue plan for his planet. Fourthly, Jesus shows us how we are to work. Jesus chose to come to a planet where work had become painful toil. Everything seemed to be against him. Even in the hardship and persecution and even despite the resulting death, Jesus' work was foremost in his life until he uttered the words "It is finished" on the cross. Imagine feeling like that about your work – however unbearable it gets, it is a call from God, and we are to endure to the end.

Vocation, vocation, vocation

We saw in the last chapter how Abraham saw his life in terms of a present vocation, not just in terms of a future location. Similarly we must make sure that we are not working primarily in order to pay off the mortgage on a dream retirement home by the sea, but because we believe that God has called us to this work. Our work, whatever we do, is a vocation from God. What is the difference between a job and a vocation? It is simply a matter of perspective.

> Slaves, obey your earthly masters in everything; and do it, not only when their eye is on you and to win their favor, but with sincerity of heart and reverence for the Lord. Whatever you do, work at it with all your heart, as working for the Lord, not for men, since you know that you will receive an inheritance from the Lord as a reward. It is the Lord Christ you are serving (Col. 3:22-24).

Same in school. do all work to the best of your ability - be a good example

These verses encourage us to see our jobs as working for God, not simply working for men. Seeing our working life as an act of worship, as a response to God's call to be his image bearers, to be the salt of the earth and the light of the world, may not actually change what we do at work. There will still be essays to mark, patients to see, shelves to stack, meals to prepare and reports to file. But it ought to change why and how we do what we do.

to all even when no one is looking

When I was sixteen, I had the most boring Saturday job in the world. They could have trained a monkey to do my job but would probably have been stopped by animal rights campaigners for neglecting the monkey's right to stimulation. I sat at a machine for hours on end, a machine which opened envelopes for me. I had to reach in to take the envelope out and if the check inside matched the amount on the bill I put it one pile. If it didn't I put it on another. As I sat there I wondered if there was anything more to this job than funding my growing addiction to CDs, books and computer hardware, I asked God how I could redeem the time. I decided on a three-pronged approach.

Firstly, I wanted to do a good job of my work, setting accuracy and speed targets for opening letters, while avoiding paper cuts and the chomping jaws of the machine. Secondly, I believed God had given me time to pray. I certainly didn't need my mind for my job, so I allowed it to work its way

around the room praying for my work colleagues and wha[t]
little I knew about their lives, and praying for opportunities to
share something of the gospel with them. I also used my time
to reflect on the week and memorize Scripture. Thirdly, I
decided I would make the most of the heavily subsidized
canteen to try and be a part of the pretty nondescript social
life of work. As I saw myself in my work for a purpose beyond
building two piles of envelopes, I felt a sense of vocation as
God's agent to reach the people in that place, to influence
the company I worked for with Kingdom values.

A friend of mine took this role very seriously and modeled
it brilliantly. She did her level best to find positive things in
her colleagues to encourage. She was very deliberate about
taking time to ask good questions and to follow up on con-
versations with people who had expressed worry or concern. She timetabled extra time into team meetings to be
able to share something of what she had been learning at
church, or to invite them to an evangelistic discussion group
she ran in the lunch hour. She acted as the pastor of her
work in a very quiet yet significant way and her colleagues
appreciated the sense of community she brought to the
office.

Idol or Idle?

There are two traps we can fall into regarding work, and the
Bible has a lot to say about both of these dangers. It is very
hard to walk a middle line, and often we can fluctuate
between them on a daily basis.

The first danger is to make work our idol. With the pressures on to work extra hours, to put in two hundred per cent
at work, and to take work home, work can sometimes creep
up on us and become more important to us than pleasing
God.

[handwritten margin notes: "...e in ...do it ...re often!"]

[handwritten margin note, vertical: "we don't work to provide for ourselves... that few God can dig that..."]

...o work more and more is complex. It has to do ...entity, as we have already considered. If our God-...se of significance related to work is blown out of ...tion, then we will want to be where the work is. We ...ant to succeed. Ambition, power, and financial factors ...influence us. Relationships at work can often become ...ery significant as we spend so much time with our work colleagues. This can affect our loyalty to God and our families. The more damaging this is to our family life, the less we want to face up to it, and work becomes our escape route. This vicious circle is difficult to break out of. Besides which, it can be very difficult to cut back on our working hours or our working commitments. Unmet targets can mean redundancy, and that can mean further damage to our relationships at home and with God.

In these circumstances, we need to remember that God is the one who provides, and that he can be trusted. We need to obey God's call on our life to put him first and keep our dependants in mind when we work. Harsh choices may need to be made: having a frank discussion with our boss, taking a demotion, going part time, living with less money, moving to a smaller house, or even changing jobs.

The story of Nebuchadnezzar in the book of Daniel is a cautionary tale for workaholics. King Nebuchadnezzar put everything he had into building his empire. He was the mighty, successful, powerful, wealthy and happy CEO of Babylon Incorporated. He had once confessed God as the rightful King in his life, but his work had overshadowed any hint of faith he had ever had. He began to worship the success of his kingdom. God sent a terrifying dream to Nebuchadnezzar that showed that his work was in vain and his life was to be cut short. A year later Nebuchadnezzar went insane and all resemblance of humanity left him. But this is not the end of the story. God in his mercy allowed Nebuchadnezzar to see the folly of his ways, and when he was finally able to worship God as the Most High, God saw fit to return Nebuchadnezzar to his former position.

The Bible has strong words for people who make work their idol, but also for those who are too idle to work. This refers not to people who cannot work, but to those that will not work. Proverbs 6 calls lazy people sluggards, and easy bait for poverty.

As a student this challenged me. I always felt that my life was too busy. But then I did the math: eight hours of work plus eight hours of sleep does not equal a whole day. In fact, I was left with eight hours to spare. This seemed plenty of time to wash, cook and eat, study the Bible, be with friends, see a movie, and play some sport. This was my first lesson in time management and I was sleeping too much. By restricting my sleep hours and being strict with my 9-5 work pattern, and my 5-1 social life (I was a student...) I could aim at a reasonably balanced life.

A while back I found out that watching television was regularly taking up a massive four hours of my day. Radical action was needed. Sometimes I check my diary and find that I am out at work several evenings in a row. Radical action is needed. Sometimes church activities seem to be taking up all of my waking hours. Radical action is needed. Work-life balance is more than a buzzword; it is walking the knife-edge between two of the devil's best-utilized traps: being idle or making an idol out of work.

Just be careful do your Best not to spend too much time doing any one thing - need to get frees sorted.

Am I in the right job?

Ask the question too often and we get analysis-paralysis Christians, who spend all their time worrying and never get on with anything. Or there are the tumbleweed Christians who never stick at a job long enough to make a difference. Facing the reality of a fallen world and the

[handwritten note at top: He has put each person in the country, city or town they live for a reason]

need to knuckle down and earn a living and serve God in the place that he has placed us can be a tough pill to swallow. We all long for the words of Eric Liddell, who was both an Olympic sprinter and a missionary to China, to echo in our working experience: "God made me for China, but he also made me fast, and when I run, I feel his pleasure." We want to feel God's pleasure in the work we do and yet every job has its degree of toil and the need for patient endurance.

Ask the question too rarely and we see stuck-in-a-rut Christians. They drift into their jobs, and stay there come what may. It is safe. It is predictable. They certainly cannot be labeled unfaithful. But, like Abraham, they need to be reminded to keep their ears open to the call of God on their lives to move on. Friends of mine toward the end of their working lives asked the question "Lord, am I in the right job?" The result was for one to take early retirement from lecturing in chemistry to become a consultant Bible translator. For another, it meant leaving behind a prospering architects' business to serve God among the poor in Africa. God does sometimes call us to leave behind our current careers and follow his lead into unknown territories. Another friend of mine left his work as an evangelist to serve God in management consultancy. An accountant from my church took a year out to go to Bible College and then went back into accountancy. I know of a couple of doctors from England and Albania who have forfeited their hard-earned salaries to reach out to their communities with the gospel.

Maybe God is asking us to examine how effective we are being for him in our current work. Are we so busy that we don't have time to invest in real relationships at work? Do we really know the joys and sorrows of the people that we work alongside? Are we fully aware of the ethical implications of the business we are involved in? Have we thought about the impact on the environment that our business practice actually makes? Are we fully up to speed with whether our work could encourage fair trade? Are we making the most of the evangelistic opportunities that our working life provides?

Work it out

Our jobs help us to be who God designed us to be: active, responsible, independent. Our jobs help us to be like God, whether we are creative or good at the day-to-day sustaining work. Our jobs help us to quietly demonstrate the truth of the gospel through our lives and daily contact with those who don't believe. We should feel that our jobs are given to us by God, and we are called into that place to do his will. Our goal as Christians is to see God as our boss, to see our ambition as quietly getting on with what we have been given to do, and to see our earnings in terms of the Kingdom. We must be careful not to let work so dominate our lives that it becomes an idol, taking away the worship that only God deserves. We must also be careful not to become lazy, but to work conscientiously. As we integrate our work with our worship, we work out our salvation "for it is God who works in you to will and to act according to his good purpose" (Phil. 2:13).

Just a minute

As you work, remember that God designed us to work, and thank him for the job satisfaction that you get. Ask him to help you see the significance of your work. When your work is tough, ask God to help you see ways in which you can serve him and bless the people around you.

Check your work. Is it becoming your idol, or are you slacking and becoming idle? Check if Monday mornings feel like a vocation, bringing out the best in you, or a provocation, bringing out the worst in you? Check your career path matches God's plan for your life, and make sure you are prepared to move on or stick it out, whichever he calls you to do.

As you get your paycheck, remember you can't serve God and money. Thank God for entrusting you with the money. Ask him to help you spend it wisely and give some of it away to people in need. Remember those who can't work for whatever reason, and as far as you are able, empower them with responsibility so they can enjoy the significance for which God made them.

Be considerate to the people around you and see yourself as their pastor, teaching them about Christ as they watch your lives and talk to you. Put your Bible in your briefcase or handbag. Use your screensaver, mouse mat or ring tone to remind you who else is watching you

As you anticipate your end of year appraisal, what-ever the results from your employer's perspective, ask yourself whether you expect to hear your Savior say: "Well done, you good and faithful servant" (Luke 19:17).

On the iPod

Working Nine to Five, Dolly Parton (RCA Records, 1980)
Finest Work Song, REM (IRS Records, 1993)
Manic Monday, The Bangles (Colombia Records, 1986)
Hard Day's Night, The Beatles (Parlophone, 1964)
Indescribable, Chris Tomlin (Sixsteps Records, 2006)

Off the shelf

Arthur Miller, *Death of a Salesman* (London: Penguin, 2000)
Mark Greene, *Thank God It's Monday* (Bletchley: Scripture Union, 2001)
Rodney Green, *90,000 Hours – Managing the World of Work* (Bletchley: Scripture Union, 2002)
Fraser Dyer, *Why Do I Do This Every Day? Finding Meaning in Your Work* (Oxford: Lion Hudson, 2005)
Alexander Hill, *Just Business* (Carlisle: Paternoster Press, 1998)

SHOP

THE DESIGNER'S LABEL

Shopaholics Anonymous

Shopping is the number one leisure activity for many people in the West today. It is among the top three favorite leisure pursuits in Great Britain. We shop to eat, shop to dress, shop to feel better, we window shop and internet shop. We even shop for exercise, I heard one pundit argue that "Shopping is the new walking." Whereas people used to go out for a Sunday afternoon stroll in the local park, we are far more likely now to meet our friends and neighbors in the local high street or supermarket.

Although we would never admit it, we could even be addicted to shopping. Many people practice retail therapy to exorcise their problems. We may joke about it, but 'shopaholism' leads to debt and its sister problems: family break-ups, depression, homelessness and even suicide.

Shopping is no longer a privileged pastime for the rich. However much disposable income we have or have not got, we all tend to spend more. It is no wonder debt-related issues are so widespread.

I shop therefore I am

Many years ago, when mobile phones were a luxury item, I heard a story about a man in a traffic jam on a motorway on a hot day. He was in a terrible rush, and this traffic jam meant that he was letting people down. After half an hour he realised that the guy in the lane parallel to him was chatting on a mobile phone. So he wound down the window and signalled to him his request to make a quick call, offering to reimburse him for the cost. The man put down his phone and a look of shame came across his face. "I'm really sorry," he said "it's not real."

Shopping is no longer about purchasing what you need in order to live; it is about seeking to buy an identity. Young people know this. There is a dress code on the streets that young people follow. When I watch new kids walk into a youth club, I can feel the other kids look them over, sizing them up like the tailors used to do in the suit shop. Kids work out their precise position in the socio-economic demographic league table by checking for the telltale signs of what trainers are on their feet and what kind of mobile phone is in their hand.

And although we may think we are past that, and immune to such trends of fashion, we just need to take a look at what we are wearing. I seriously doubt that you are reading this sporting 1970s flared trousers, a ra-ra skirt or a top hat. No doubt you don't raise any eyebrows walking down the street, because you fit in with everyone else. Like the kids in the youth group, we know how to conform.

Image is everything

Very slowly, we are all being brainwashed by the advertising industry, an industry dedicated to creating a desire and then showing us which shop to buy from to fulfill that need. Wherever we look, on the TV, sides of buildings, the back of bus tickets, in our newspapers and magazines, or on the football pitch, we are constantly being told what to buy. Advertising often actually tells us very little about the product being sold, because they know that image is everything. They use words and branding and pictures to create an ethos, a dream lifestyle that their product is of course an essential part of.

We looked in the last chapter about how our jobs of work often define who we are. But it is also becoming increasingly true that we define ourselves by what we buy. Shopping has become a way of making an identikit picture of ourselves so that we can make ourselves more presentable, worthy of respect.

Spending power

This is true even in the supermarket. Imagine I am standing at the checkout with a bottle of a supermarket own-brand value cola, a microwave meal for one and some anti-lice shampoo. I would be trying not to look like a lonely, para-site-ridden cheapskate, and hoping not to bump into any-body I know. In the queue behind me is a well-dressed man loading onto the conveyor belt two bottles of champagne, six large deli items neatly packaged with expensive price labels clearly showing and a huge tub of Haagen Daazs ice cream. Going through the mind of the checkout assistant is a picture of the rest of this person's life. From these nine items, we all imagine his fast car, large house and beautiful girlfriend. Of course the lifestyle isn't included when we buy these items, but to all intents and purposes the man behind me in the queue would feel quite gratified by the respect he is being shown by those around, while I am trying to sneak out the back door.

A friend of mine had a Saturday job as a sandwich board boy. He was paid to walk around town with a wooden sign on his front and his back. He was a courageous lad and had no shame walking around the busiest part of trendy Brighton bumping into his peers while advertising the local leather jacket outlet. His so-called friends used to follow him around, jeering and making fun of him. Of course it was rather degrad-ing being a walking advertisement, but the irony was that he was not the only walking advertisement in town that day. His friends were sporting labels for half the other shops in that part of town. The difference was that he was getting paid for it, while the rest of his schoolmates were paying over the odds for the privilege. He was the shrewd one of the lot of us.

Society labels us trendy or trashy, worthy of respect or a laughing stock. We can often go along with what society says without thinking. Christians are not automatically immune to such brainwashing. How can Christians honor God by refusing to conform to the spirit of this age even as we buy our groceries, furniture, cars and houses? If shopping and identity are linked as the media show us they are, then the Bible has a huge amount to teach us about how to shop.

Made in the image of God

> Then God said, "Let us make man in our image, in our likeness, and let them rule over the fish of the sea and the birds of the air, over the livestock, over all the earth, and over all the creatures that move along the ground."
>
> So God created man in his own image,
> in the image of God he created him;
> male and female he created them (Gen. 1:26-27).

Human beings, according to these verses right at the beginning of the Bible, were made to represent God in the world. We were supposed to be living examples of God's character in the way that we ruled over creation as his ambassadors. Society values us because what we do for a job, the amount of power we have, the consumer choices we make, our intelligence, and our physical attractiveness. Being made in the image of God gives human beings intrinsic value. We are valuable because of who made us and because of whom we represent.

He is no artist. He has not had any classical training, he doesn't have an eye for color and he certainly has no awareness of perspective, lighting or composition. And yet my home and my office are full of his artwork. His artwork is valuable to me because the artist is my son. We may not possess much about us that could be called talented or beautiful, and yet God sees value in us because he made us.

A friend of mine has never been allowed to forget the time when he was invited for tea as a child. He was seated at the table and was told that tuna pasta bake was being served. His reply, as his parents frequently reminded him, was, "It's not that I dislike pasta . . . I detest it." You can imagine the look of horror on the host's face. Unfortunately we often act like this toward God. We are fearfully and wonderfully made by an awesome Creator, but when we look in the mirror often all we see are our so-called flaws. God also made the birds and the flowers and the animals. However, we are told that we are infinitely more valuable than the birds of the air or the flowers in the field, because only human beings bear the image of God.

A human being is worthy of respect and honor, no matter what race, culture, gender or social class they are from because they represent God. If we intend to love the Lord our God with all our heart, soul and mind then we will love our neighbor as ourselves, caring for them body, soul and mind. Whatever we do for the least significant person, we do as worship to God. Knowing that we represent God cannot lead to selfish individualism or narcissism because at the same time that we affirm our own value, we affirm the value of every human being on the planet.

God made us in his image, which means we are supposed to display God's character through our words, thoughts and deeds, but we all fail in this role, failing to represent God as we should. As Paul writes in the letter to the church in Rome: "We have all fallen short of the glory of God." So instead of displaying the true character of God we often display a living contradiction of God's nature: selfishness not selflessness, hate not love, sinfulness not holiness, war not peace.

Christ the image of God

God sent Jesus into the world to be his true image-bearer. Hebrews 1 says that the "Son is the radiance of the Father's glory and bears his exact representation." Jesus does what we should have done, in that he perfectly portrays the character of God in all that he does. He is the second Adam representing the perfection of God's character in the face of severe persecution and opposition. Then this perfect image of God willingly carries the stain and the shame of our sins. In Jesus' willingness to lay down his life as a sacrifice for our sins, we see the compassion, grace and mercy of God. In Christ's death on the cross we have another angle on our identity and significance. We can understand our value in the eyes of God by the price that he was willing to pay to purchase us.

Every time we acquiesce to the media's insistence that we are significant because of the car we drive, the shoes we wear, or the grades we get at school we are saying to God that these things are more important than what Jesus did for us.

Imagine a father laboring away in the garage, making a wooden rocking horse for his daughter's birthday. Night after night he slaves away at it trying to get it ready for the big day. He has invested time, energy and money into this effort. He is eagerly looking forward to the day when he can set in front of his child and see the look on her face as she unwraps it. The big day arrives; she opens his present and mumbles a thank you before pushing it aside. Then her face lights up at a plastic doll that her friend has bought her. Imagine the father's heart. How infinitely more disappointing for God who made the world for us, sent his own Son to die for us, and gave us the opportunity for eternal life. What makes our faces light up are new shoes and mobile phones, cars and houses. Often we are more joyful over a new purchase that comes in a plastic bag than over God's purchase of our freedom at the cost of his own Son.

Transformed to the image of Christ

When we become Christians God fills us with his Spirit and begins a transforming process to make us more and more like Jesus who is himself the image of the invisible God. So we are restored to our original role of being the image-bearers of God. Jesus has succeeded where we failed and he has bought for us the right to have the privilege of demonstrating God's character to the watching universe. One day God's transforming work in us will be complete and in heaven we will perfectly demonstrate the character of God as God intended.

Whenever the world says to us "You are what you own" we need to remember that God says "You are not your own – you were bought at a price" (1 Cor. 6:19-20). Shopping for Christians should not be a matter of updating our identity for the benefit of a watching world. We are valuable already because of who made us, who we represent and because of the price that someone was willing to pay for us. However, shopping for Christians should be for the benefit of a watching world in three distinct areas.

Throwing it all away

We live in a disposable society; if something breaks it is more often than not cheaper and easier to buy a new one than to have it fixed. We buy our kids presents and when they break, we no longer say "Don't worry – I'll fix it", we say: "Don't worry – I'll order you a new one on the internet."

Relationships have become disposable too. Rather than spend time working problems through it is becoming more acceptable and easier to dispose of the broken relationship and start a fresh one. Our attitude to church can be a bit like choosing a shampoo. We will stick with it until it doesn't do the job for us anymore, then we will switch to a new one.

Christians need to be challenged by God's commitment to the human race. We betrayed God and yet rather than dispose of us, God went to great cost to repair the damage. God's commitment to us as a human race has been restoration rather than rejection. We need to learn to exhibit the faithful character of God in the face of a disposable society. We need to learn to be committed to God in the good times and in the difficult times. We need to learn to be committed to other people for better or for worse, because that is how our God is committed to us.

Christians need to stand out as those unwilling to conform to a disposable society. Let us show loyalty in our relationships. Let us not treat church and family like a commodity that can be returned or exchanged. Let's be careful of what we dispose of. Let us protect the environment by leading the way in ecofriendly consumer habits.

Pay nothing until February

I was never frustrated waiting for public transport until I went to European cities. The transport there is frequent, regular, predictable and punctual. I got used to never having to wait more than a few minutes. So when I returned to England, I turned into Mr Impatient. It's like that with shopping: with so much on offer instantly, waiting for anything makes us more impatient than ever. Our society encourages instant personal gratification. The "I want it and I want it now" spoilt child syndrome is visible everywhere. We shop for fast food and shop with instant credit. We never have to wait to afford something before we buy it. We can buy now, and pay later.

God is patient. As we read the accounts in the Bible of the nation of Israel, we learn that God was long-suffering with his people. In our own lives, God has started a long-term process in us that will not be complete until heaven. We enjoy in this time a foretaste of the kingly reign of God in our lives but not its fulfilment. The whole world is groaning, waiting to be renewed. And so the Christian life is one of longing and of delayed gratification. This means that we learn not to expect perfection in this life, but understand there will be suffering, pain, and disappointment but there is hope that one day all things will be put right. We need to exhibit the godly characteristics of patience and compassion.

. Zacchaeus was known to be a swindler, prepared to betray his countrymen and steal from them, until he experienced Jesus' unconditional acceptance. From that moment on his personal gratification turned into prolific generosity. Let us follow his example, asking not how much we can get but how much we can give. Let us seek justice and equity above personal accumulation. Let us learn to be patient and compassionate in our spending.

Spending habit

The advertisers have got a problem. They want to sell us a product based on the assumption that they can make us believe it is the missing thing in our life. But they do not actually want the product to provide what is missing in our life because then we won't want to buy anything else. So the products being advertised never live up to expectations because we did not really want it in the first place and because the advertisers need to maintain room to create more desire.

Despite this problem, the advertisers seem to have us hooked. We are easily fooled into thinking that we are dysfunctional until we can get our hands on whatever they are showing us. A teacher once told me advertisers teach children to read. When I tried it out on my pre-school children, I was shocked to find out that they could indeed "read" the words "McDonalds" "Coca-Cola" and "Cadburys." Not only that, they also were also easily able to express that they wanted what the logos represented. Unfortunately I am no better. I find it difficult to drive past a Ferrari dealership without gawping.

Philippians 4 tells us that Paul had learned to be content whatever his circumstances. This was not something that came naturally, but in his experience of great riches and plenty and also of severe poverty and hardship, he had learned the secret of contentment: 'I can do everything through him who gives me strength.'

Paul's words to the Philippian church are vital for us to hear today. We worship whatever we are willing to sacrifice for. Many people sacrifice their family time or their church involvement for the trappings of status and success. Their spending habits betray whom they are really worshipping. We know we cannot worship money and Jesus but many of us are trying very hard anyway.

Shop 'til you drop

Jesus is not opposed to personal property. Christians should not be banned from shopping. But in a culture where shopping and possessions have become the god of many people around us, we need a new approach to shopping. Jesus' teaching on money and possessions is particularly difficult for us to swallow and we need to recognise the battle between commitment and disposability, compassion and desire, contentment and dissatisfaction. Our last purchase will inevitably be our own coffin and our last will and testament will ultimately give all we own away free of charge. Jesus made that point very clear in the story of the man who received a windfall, bought bigger barns and whose life was held accountable before God within twenty-four hours. We need to learn to spend ourselves in worship to God and for the benefit of others in this life.

Just a minute

Look back over last month's bank statements and evaluate your purchases. What did you buy that you needed? What did you buy that you wanted? What did you buy on impulse? What did you buy for somebody else? What would Jesus say about your bank statement? Would you be embarrassed if your neighbor saw it, or a third-world church pastor saw it? How could you have better spent or saved your money? Check that the advertisers are not influencing your decisions. Avoid designer labels if possible. Thank God for the products you buy. Be generous and buy something for somebody else. Recognise those in need around you – buy *The Big Issue* or put your change in the charity boxes. Avoid instant credit. Buy items that are fairly traded. Avoid items with superfluous amounts of packaging. Refuse or reuse plastic carrier bags. Fix things occasionally, or freecycle them. Fast from shopping – one day a week, one weekend a month or one month of the year.

On the iPod

Bitter Sweet Symphony, The Verve (Hut, 1997)
Money, Money, Money, Abba (Polar Music, 1976)
I Will Offer Up My Life, Matt Redman (Survivor Records, 1998)
Material Girl, Madonna (Sire Records, 1984)
When I Survey the Wondrous Cross, Isaac Watts (1707)

Off the shelf

Graham Cheesman, *Hyperchoice* (Leicester: IVP, 1997)
Naomi Klein, *No Logo* (London: Flamingo, 2001)
Ronald J. Sider, *Rich Christians In An Age of Hunger* (Nashville: Word Publishing, 2005)
Pete Ward, *Selling Worship* (Milton Keynes: Authentic, 2005)
Richard Foster, *Freedom In Simplicity* (Grand Rapids, Zondervan, 2005)

COOK

GENEROUS SERVINGS

Food, glorious food

I have it on the highest scientific authority (a napkin from the London Science Museum) that in our lifetimes we will consume food the equivalent in weight of nine elephants. I wonder if I could actually buy nine elephants (there is probably a bulk discount) and store them in a massive freezer in my garage? I could have rasher of trunk for breakfast, rump steak for lunch, leg chop for tea and tail crackling nibbles for my mid-morning snack. It would certainly save on all the hassle of going to the shops, deciding what to cook, chopping, dicing, frying, garnishing, serving out, keeping things hot and washing up. Just think how much of our time is spent shopping and preparing, eating and clearing away food.

Why didn't God just make little tablets that we could swallow that would give us all the nutrients and vitamins we needed for a week, or a food patch that we could stick on our arms so that nutrition could be introduced by osmosis into our blood supply? When God designed us to need nourishment, God loved us enough to give us taste buds and to provide food that would stimulate them.

The picture of the Garden of Eden is of a wonderful place with amazing food. God made food that not only tasted good but was good to look at too. God invented strawberries, bananas and pineapples, and gave us the creativity to learn to make chocolate out of the cocoa beans. When God hid sugar in canes and flour in wheat, God expected us to discover culinary potential. When God told humanity to rule over the world, he meant for us to order it and use it creatively. The cultural mandate implied the creation of curries and sorbets, pies and fajitas. They are the outworking of God, encouraging us to enjoy his good creation.

Recipe for disaster

But that is not the whole story. Food is good but it can always go bad. It is fascinating that God chose food as the area in which the first humans could prove or disprove their loyalty to their loving Creator. God could have made a forbidden place, word, thought or activity, but in his wisdom, he chose a forbidden fruit. God wanted human beings to be different from the animals, ruling over their desires rather than being ruled by them. Human beings had to choose whether they would trust God over their senses and obey him or whether they would follow their stomachs. Eating the forbidden fruit was a recipe for disaster. It was an act of rebellion against God and a cry of independence and so God gave human beings a taste of what independence from him would be like. Because we did not fight our appetites but allowed them to rule over us, we now have to fight nature in order to feed ourselves.

> Cursed is the ground because of you;
> through painful toil you will eat of it
> all the days of your life.
> It will produce thorns and thistles for you,
> and you will eat the plants of the field (Gen. 3:17-18).

This curse not only brought about weeds, nettles and brambles but also introduced hunger and famine, as nature was no longer on our side. Most of us experience this battle with nature every day.

Table manners

Some people are too busy to eat. That was not how God intended life to be: if we are too busy to eat properly then we are too busy. We should slow down enough to trust God that he has given us enough time to do his will and that includes caring for our bodies by eating correctly.

Some people are so affected by what other people think of their bodies that they will not eat. Remember what we looked at in the last chapter. We are made in the image of God and therefore we are valuable however we look. We should enjoy God's provision of food and not reject his care for us.

Some people are so ruled by their desires that they don't control what they eat. They never say no to second helpings, raid the fridge regularly, ignore the nutritional information on the packets or snack secretly between meals. In the Garden of Eden what Adam and Eve ate was an opportunity to show God that he was first in their lives. Similarly we must watch what we eat so that food does not rule over us.

We want to learn how to bring worship to God in a fallen world through our interaction with food. Paul writing to Christians on how they handled food offered to idols wrote: "whether you eat or drink or whatever you do, do it all for the glory of God" (1 Cor. 10:31). Choosing whether to eat meat offered to idols became worship to God through respect of the consciences of other people and through God-pleasing motives. Issues around cooking and eating still contain areas of massive controversy, choice and conscience. Yet Paul's guidance still rings true that we can do it all for God's glory. Food and drink provides opportunities to bring us closer to each other and to God.

Compliments to the chef

When my daughter was seven months old, I wanted to patent a new method of training bomb disposal experts. In order to help them learn precision, accuracy, and hand-eye coordination, I proposed they visit me at teatime and try their hand at feeding the baby. I had to wait for that split-second window of opportunity to get the heavily-laden spoon past her wildly flailing arms and into her open mouth, aiming it just right to get some deep enough on her tongue so she swallowed it rather than spat it right back at me. It would be great training for any field agent. It was almost a lost cause, but I persevered because feeding is bonding. I was always jealous of the connection my wife enjoyed with our children as she breastfed them. Breastfeeding was more than providing food: it offered comfort, warmth and love to my children and made my wife feel needed and indispensable. In the short time between breast milk and a child's mealtime independence there is an opportunity where fathers can be involved in feeding and I was determined not to miss out.

God wants us to bond with him as he feeds us. That was the lesson of the people of God in the desert. When Moses looked back over the forty years the Israelites were in the desert after their escape from Egyptian slavery, he told the people that the whole point of God's provision in the wilderness was for bonding, so that the people of Israel would understand that food is an opportunity to understand and express their dependence on God. Just as my daughter was reliant on me to provide her food, she was also reliant on my love that motivated me to feed her. Similarly in the desert God feeds his people, teaching them to depend on his provision and his word of promise that proves reliable every day. Moses understood this when he wrote: "man does not live on bread alone but on every word comes from the mouth of the Lord" (Deut. 8:3). This same sense of dependence on God for our daily food is expressed in the Lord's Prayer, where we are told to pray "give us this day our daily bread", and in Proverbs 30:8,9: "Keep falsehood and lies far from me; give me neither poverty nor riches, but give me only my daily bread. Otherwise, I may have too much and disown you and say, 'Who is the LORD?' Or I may become poor and steal, and so dishonor the name of my God."

The writer is echoing the concerns Moses had for his people who, after spending forty years in the desert learning to rely on God, were in danger of forgetting the Lord when they entered the Promised Land where food would be plentiful (Deut. 8). The antidote to this danger was thanksgiving and the same is true for us. We live in a land of plenty and we can easily forget it is not simply due to Sainsbury's farmers and Tesco's packers that we have enough to eat. God who set up our world to be hospitable to life continues to sustain it, providing enough food for the whole planet (although we have not distributed it fairly). Giving thanks for our food is a way of acknowledging our dependence on God and expressing our gratitude.

I am not suggesting a meaningless exercise of reciting well-worn words that we trot out without engaging our minds before every mealtime. For many of us 'saying grace' has become a chore. Sometimes it seems that a prayer such as "For what we are about to receive, may the Lord make us truly grateful" is little more than a glorified permission to begin eating. It is also an insult to the cook as it implies that there is no way we would be grateful for the food before us without supernatural empowerment.

We need to foster an attitude of gratitude for our food and it is good to be in the habit of saying thank you to God. This can be done in a spontaneous and creative way, before, during or after the meal. We can use meal times as an opportunity to punctuate our day with prayer, being thankful not just for the food, but for all the ways God has provided for us. The discussions over the meal table may well raise issues that you could bring to God after the meal.

God is our Provider and it is good to remember him. If you are the provider of food for your family never underestimate this opportunity to draw close to God or represent God.

When I was pastoring my church, I was called to be a shepherd to draw attention to Jesus the good Shepherd. The same is true for those who cook, as they are providing food for others and thereby pointing people to *Jehovah Jireh* "the Lord who provides."

Eat your greens

Those of us who do most of the shopping and cooking for the family are often under-appreciated, but even this disappointing let down is a great opportunity to connect with God. How many times has God worked to provide something for us and yet we have been too stubborn to accept or too thoughtless to say thank you. When our family is ungrateful or our kids just won't eat the meal we've slaved over, we can ask that God would use these times to teach us about his often-unappreciated faithfulness to us. Pray that when we make hard decisions about healthy food and all we get are grumbles, the experience would make our hearts more receptive to the times when God says no to things we want because he wants to give us the things we really need.

Many people feel rejected when their kids, spouses, parents or houseguests reject the meals they have cooked. This is because providing food involves time, love, care and consideration and the recipient should see this behind any overcooked greens or burned toppings. When our meals are pushed away half-eaten or hardly touched, without any sign of appreciation, we can bring our disappointment to our Heavenly Father. Through this we draw closer to him who continues to provide for us his enduring love even though we spurn his good gifts to us every day.

How many of us would think of painting a rock to look like a loaf of bread just to watch our guests break their teeth? How many of us, instead of giving a child a boiled egg for breakfast, would consider that a live venomous snake would be more entertaining (Matt. 7:9-12)? None of us would dare to play with the health of those we feed in this way because we are not only demonstrating our love for those round the table, but we are also expecting trust. We should be developing the same trust for God as those we provide food for have for us.

God, the host

I remember visiting my older female cousins when I was a boy. They were eleven and thirteen and I saw them as the source of all wisdom regarding the opposite sex. Their key piece of advice to me, a ten year old, was ... "Whatever you do, don't take a girl out for food on the first date. You are bound to slurp, or to spill something; you might drool or drop some food from your mouth. Eating together is a no-no." God has the complete opposite view on relationships and food. In the Bible eating is essentially a social activity. Eating breaks down barriers because it is hard to be formal when you are slurping and chewing. Eating brings people together, because we find it easier to relate to others as we engage in a common activity. We all need to eat and we all need to meet. God combines these two needs in three holy meals described in the Bible: the fellowship offering, the final banquet and the Lord's Supper.

In Leviticus 3 God invites worshippers to a meal with him. The fellowship offering was given by God to help people express their appreciation of him, celebrating the completion of a vow or just their gratitude to God. Part of the meat was to be offered to God, the rest to be shared in a holy meal. The Jewish people were not just saying grace but eating it. Taking part in eating the meal was God's chosen way of asking for worship from his people.

God does not want to be at arm's distance, aloof and unattainable: he wants to be intimate with us, to draw close to us and eat with us. This should be more shocking for us than if the Monarch of England were to suddenly turn up to tea tonight. Jesus, King of Kings, insists that he wants to eat with us. What a privilege, an honor and a pleasure.

The book of Revelation kicks off with seven letters to seven churches. To the lukewarm Christians that make Jesus feel like he needs to be sick, Christians whose love and intimacy have become tepid, he says: "I stand at the door and knock. If anyone hears my voice and opens the door, I will come in and eat with him, and he with me." (Rev. 3:20). Jesus is offering a way back to intimacy with him, by picturing relationship with him as sharing a meal together. This is an incredible privilege. Jesus wants to relate to us like one of the family members around the dinner table. God calls in on us to share food together: eating in God's company is worship.

Dinner invitation

As Christians we fail every week in our discipleship, we fail to live as Jesus did, loving the lost and the excluded. Despite this failure, Jesus still invites us to join him for a meal. The Lord's Supper is a dinner for sinners. When we eat the bread and drink the wine, we remember that if it were not for our sin, Jesus would not have needed to die. We remember that God loved us enough to let his own Son die for us so that we might know the intimacy of sharing a meal with God. The Lord's Supper is a meal with a message. It reaffirms to us the seriousness of our sin and yet the depth of God's love for us. Because we ate the forbidden fruit and turned our backs on God, Jesus had to drink the cup of God's wrath to take the penalty we deserve. Jesus drank the cup of God's wrath in order that we could drink the cup of fellowship. Jesus prepared the ultimate fellowship offering for us by offering himself as a sacrifice for us and then offering us the symbols of his body and blood in the bread and wine as a worshipful meal. Christians should not turn down God's invitation to share this meal on a regular basis.

The Lord's Supper is a vital meal but it is not the most important meal of the week. Jesus has more to say about caring for the poor, feeding the hungry, and accepting the stranger than he does about the Lord's Supper. If we are not following the Lord's commands the rest of the week, then following the Lord's command on the Lord's Supper is no substitute.

In the 1967 film *Guess Who's Coming to Dinner*, Spencer Tracy and Katherine Hepburn play a wealthy white couple who are told that their daughter's fiancé is coming to meet them, and that he is black. This film appeared when interracial marriage was shocking and the film challenged attitudes of the day. If the film were to be remade today, it would probably be rich parents meeting their daughter's boyfriend who is a convict on parole.

Inviting someone to sit down at the family dining table is letting them right into the heart of our home. Inviting someone to sit down at the family dining table for Christmas dinner is effectively letting them know they are accepted as part of the family. In Jesus' day most meals had this kind of social significance. At that time you were not what you ate, but who you ate with. Then the Pharisees were the most religiously devout group and they reacted against compromising religious leaders in Israel that had offered sacrifices to pagan gods. The Pharisees encouraged people to live more holy lives and to voluntarily submit to the priestly laws of ritual purity. This put a lot of emphasis on what you ate and with whom. The Pharisees would only eat ritually clean food with ritually clean people for fear of becoming defiled themselves. This is why they were so upset with Jesus and his disciples' attitude to food and friends: Jesus' disciples did not wash their hands before eating (Matt. 15:10-11). Jesus attended too many dinner parties and so was branded a glutton and drunk (Matt. 11:19). But even worse, Jesus had all the wrong kinds of dinner guests (Luke 15:1-2).

Jesus broke the rules of decorum and decency of his day by inviting all the wrong kind of people to share a meal with him. I have no doubt that today Jesus would have dinner with the freemasons and the asylum seekers. He would choose to eat in the soup kitchens and school canteens. Consider what we know about Zacchaeus the corrupt tax inspector. I imagine that no one had been round to dinner with Zacchaeus for a long time: tax collectors were social outcasts, collaborators, the most despised people in Israel. So when Zacchaeus is seen up a tree secretly trying to get a glimpse of the man everyone is talking about, Jesus walks straight up to him and, in front of everyone, tells him that he is coming to his house for tea. All the people mutter that Jesus has gone to be the guest of a sinner and this simple act of Jesus' compassion, coupled with Jesus' teaching convicts Zacchaeus to change his ways. Jesus dined with the despised because Jesus came to save the lost, to treat the sick, and to show unconditional love to the unlovely. If we are to be godly people, we need to start eating with the ungodly; sharing our tables with the wrong sort of people to show them the right way to God.

Jesus is no social spoilsport: he encourages his disciples to throw dinner parties. But these are to be meals with a meaning which express God's priorities. Jesus even gave rules about the guest list. He told us we should invite the sick and disabled who, in Jesus' day, would have been beggars because there was no welfare state. They were the people often treated as subhuman and branded under the curse of God, losers and drop-outs. Jesus wants these kinds of people to be our dinner guests because he wants to turn upside down the wisdom of the world and demonstrate his transforming grace around our meal tables. Jesus wants to break barriers down and show that it does not matter about your economic or social standing in the eyes of God. Jesus' teaching on dinner parties shows a radically different agenda to the world around us. Jesus wants us to demonstrate that the things that divide people in the world today do not exclude them from the love of God. He asks not just that we mix together in the church services, but that we mix it up around the dining table.

We are told not to invite friends, family and rich neighbors for fear of doing it just to get invited back (Luke 14:12-14). Many of us live as if this is the whole point of dinner parties and get offended if we are never invited back. The ethics of the Kingdom do not operate on this kind of social exchange structure. Our God is a God of grace who does not have a you-scratch-my-back-I'll-scratch-yours mentality or a you-do-some-good-works-then-I'll-let-you-into-heaven system. We can never repay God for his grace and mercy. Instead God asks us to emulate that grace by providing dinner parties on earth which are mouth-watering *hors d'oeuvres*, whetting people's appetites for the ultimate messianic banquet in heaven.

A hearty appetite

Am I making you hungry as you read this? Have you licked your lips while reading this chapter? We need to eat because we get hungry and the hunger we experience can be a reminder to express and experience worship to God. C.S. Lewis[1] argued that we hunger because food really exists to satisfy our hunger; we thirst because water really exists to slake our thirst. We can see in ourselves and in humanity the world over a hunger for God and a desire to worship, because God exists to satisfy our need for him. Jesus affirms this just after he has fed the five thousand. He describes himself as the bread of life and tells the Samaritan woman that what she is really thirsty for in life can only be satisfied by a relationship with him.

The Bible teaches that we can use physical hunger as a means to create a greater hunger for God. Fasting is a way of expressing our allegiance to God, a way of telling him that he comes first in our lives. A spouse or a parent who turns down a strategic promotion at work because they want to spend more time with their family signals that relationships come higher up on their list of priorities than earning money or making a name. So with fasting we are giving up a legitimate need in our life in order to express to God that he comes first. Fasting is a way of saying to God that we want our desire for him to rule over the other desires in our lives. Fasting is a way of using our physical hunger for food as an alarm clock to awaken our hunger for God.

Our approach to food can also be an opportunity to show faithfulness to God. This is significant in understanding Daniel's decision to say "No" to King Nebuchadnezzar's royal food and wine and to eat vegetables and drink water for three years. Daniel and his friends did not want their passion for God to be weakened through choice foods. Daniel knew that his heart was vulnerable and that if he got attached to the high life he might not be able to let it go. We need to learn self-control in what we eat so that we will not let food rule over us. Saying "Yes" to food is the natural response, as we see in the animal kingdom. Our humanity is proved when we say no to our appetites and exercise self-control. Saying "No" to food in order to say "Yes" to God takes passion. Fasting is costly worship; it is more difficult than turning up at church services and singing a few choruses. However we must also keep fasting in its proper context:

Is not this the kind of fasting I have chosen:
to loose the chains of injustice
and untie the cords of the yoke,
to set the oppressed free
 and break every yoke?
Is it not to share your food with the hungry
and to provide the poor wanderer with shelter—
when you see the naked, to clothe him,
and not to turn away from your own flesh and blood?

(Isa. 58:6-7).

Even the costly worship of fasting is meaningless if it is not accompanied with a compassion for the needy. We live in a hungry world, where our livestock are subsidised by more money than seventy-five per cent of Africans have to live on.[2] The statistics are shameful. We were all told as children when we left food on our plate to remember those with no food on theirs. Yet Jesus went to parties and ate and drank, and was labeled a glutton – not a grumpy prophet berating people because of world poverty. It was this same Jesus who lived a life of selfless generosity. We need this balance in our Christian lives: a generosity to the poor and yet a celebration and thankfulness of God's good gifts. Simple steps like making a conscious decision to buy more fairly traded food, supporting charities seeking to bring emergency relief to the starving, and modeling a healthy and disciplined appetite are relatively easy steps that God may use for his glory alongside our dinner parties and sheer enjoyment of good food.

Just a minute

God wants to bond with us as he feeds us. Accept food from him with an attitude of gratitude and become more like God your Provider, as you provide for others.

God wants our company as he enjoys the intimacy of eating with us. Acknowledge God's presence and provision when you eat, and make the most of the Lord's Supper to draw closer to God regularly.

God wants us to show his grace face to face by the way that we share our food with the needy. Intercontinental food parcels are not enough. Deliberately invite people for dinner that you do not get on so well with at work, church or in your road. Next time someone asks you for money on the street, buy them some food.

God is what our hearts were made for: he is the food we hunger for. Remember that when your stomach rumbles. Fast regularly, sensibly and quietly to reinforce this point to your body. Use the time freed up from cooking, eating and clearing up in prayer and service to others. Give away the money you would have spent on those meals.

In order to help cooking time become enriching-relationship-with-God time, make the most of inviting friends, neighbors and work colleagues to share meals with you. Beans on toast can make for good, honest conversation, without etiquette getting in the way. A three-course extravaganza gives plenty of time and food for thought. Take any excuse to be hospitable: birthdays, anniversaries, Christmas, Chinese New Year, or even some good weather. Be creative. Experiment with taste, color and texture. Try new ingredients and recipes. Enjoy family meals together. Use a table regularly. Switch off the television during meals or don't answer the telephone. Encourage everyone to participate in conversation over the table. Accept invitations graciously. When you are eating alone, imagine God himself sitting with you and enjoying your meal and your company.

On your iPod

Hungry, Brian Doerkson (Vineyard Music, 1999)
Guide Me, O Thou Great Jehovah, William Williams (1745)
Chocolate, Snow Patrol (Fiction Records, 2004)
Harvest For the World, The Isley Brothers (T-Neck Records, 1976)
Scenes From an Italian Restaurant, Billy Joel (Colombia Records, 1977)

Off the shelf

Conrad Gempf, *Mealtime Habits of the Messiah* (Grand Rapids: Zondervan, 2005)
John Piper, *A Hunger For God* (Leicester: IVP, 1997)
Jamie Oliver, *The Naked Chef* (London: Penguin, 2001)
Eric Schlosser, *Fast Food Nation* (London: Penguin, 2002)
Joanne Harris, *Chocolat* (London: Black Swan, 2000)

Notes

[1] C.S. Lewis, *Weight of his Glory in Transposition and other addresses* (London: Geoffrey Bles, 1949), p.25.
[2] Jessica Williams, *Fifty Facts That Should Change the World* (Cambridge: Icon Books, 2004), p.46.

FAMILY

IT'S ALL RELATIVE

Theory of Relativity

Every time Wimbledon comes around, the public tennis courts behind my home, usually neglected and wasted space, suddenly become alive with activity. Most of the year we have sole use of them for teaching small children cycling proficiency, but during those few weeks in June we can't get anywhere near them, partly because of the queue of budding tennis players we suddenly acquire in the neighborhood, and partly because of the danger of stray flying tennis balls. Wimbledon brings out the tennis player in all of us. It becomes the big discussion topic with the neighbors. Also during these two weeks of the year, my definition of family broadens. I claim to be a relative of Tim Henman – one of the best tennis players in Britain. He is somehow related to my wife's father's father's sister's son's wife's sister. I think.

But extended family members are not always so welcome. When I was sixteen, I spent the summer with my Dad's family in Malaysia, armed for the long holiday with a promising book called *The Practice of Godliness* by Jerry Bridges. However, every time I picked up the book, I was whisked off to another family engagement, meeting relatives that I did not know existed and that were even more tenuously related to me than Tim Henman. I was frustrated. I was bored with smiling politely and making small talk. All these relatives: why couldn't I just get some peace to read my book? Then it struck home. I was learning about the practice of godliness practically – in my family. This transformed the way I spent that holiday. With each new family relationship discovered, I saw an opportunity to practice showing God's character. Time with family became worship of God for me that summer when I had no time, peace or space for quiet time.

For some of us, family and the commitments that entails may be a great source of pleasure and pride. For others, family and family responsibilities may be a source of frustration and pain. For most of us, family is an intense combination of the two. What the Bible says about family resonates with our experience and helps us to see the time we spend with our relatives as a call on our lives and integral to our worship of our God.

Head of the family

Which is the first family mentioned in the Bible? Adam and Eve? There is a family mentioned even before the first human family. Genesis 1:1 says "In the beginning God . . ." Before there ever was a human family there was a heavenly family. God is a family – Father, Son and Holy Spirit – the Trinity. This means that fam-ily is a divine concept. Of course God is not genetically the Father of Jesus, no sexual relations took place and Jesus has always existed. Fatherhood, as defined by God, is relationship.

This is incredibly reassuring in today's complicated families where step-parenting, single parenting, fostering, adoption, mislabeled IVF embryos, and DNA paternity tests cause confusion for many of us regarding our identity. We can still be mothers and fathers to children not biologically ours because God models a loving parental relationship as the true definition of fatherhood. Blood may be thicker than water, but unconditional love shown in relationship is even thicker still. This fact alone draws worship from the apostle Paul, who writes: "For this reason I kneel before the Father, from whom his whole family in heaven and on earth derives its name" (Eph. 3:14-15).

God's Fatherhood is to be the source of our understanding of all fatherhood. This is hard to accept for those who feel that they cannot trust God as Father because they grew up with a father who abused, mistreated or misunderstood them. Reassuringly, our understanding of God as our Father is not a projection of our own earthly fathers. Rather our heavenly Father is the perfect example of fatherhood against which all natural fathers fall short. More than that, God's family love is the benchmark for all family relationships. As a father, I need to aspire to the fatherhood of God. As a son, I need to reflect the sonship of Jesus. As a family member, I need to reflect the family interdependence of the Trinity.

God did not create human beings because the Trinity family relationship was insufficient. God was not lonely; he had the most perfect and fulfilling relationship it is possible to have. God has always existed as Trinity, a community of personalities yet one in essence, not just showing love, but being love. It is in this context that he created the human race.

The Trinity is a very difficult concept to grasp. One often used illustration is that I, one person can describe myself in three ways – as a son, a brother and a father. This helps, but it is still insufficient for understanding God in Trinity. God is not simply one Person with three roles, but three Persons as one God. God has deliberately chosen to define himself as three persons using relational concepts, and this should impact our understanding of family as a unified togetherness that reflects God's love and care to each other. In a culture where family seems to have diminishing significance, as Christians we need to emulate and live up to this high calling of family.

Family breakdown

If God is the first family mentioned in the Bible, Adam and Eve are the second generation in the family tree. They were modeled on God and his likeness and designed to show the world God's love in relationship. The only thing that God declared not good in his perfect world was isolation and loneliness. An independent solitary human life did not fit God's intention for creation. Together man and woman were to represent God. There was an inbuilt relationship: Eve was created out of Adam. They were literally made for each other.

Family life was planned by God to bring support and companionship for one another. But what happened? The first family had the first family breakdown. Instead of supporting one another to serve God, family life became an opportunity to team up against God. Instead of encouraging each other to be faithful to their heavenly Father they tempted one another and led one another astray. And as Genesis unfolds, we see how this affected everything – their relationship with God, their relationship with each other as they ran to hide and cover themselves up, and their relationship with children and grandchildren. Adam blamed his disobedience on God for creating Eve and part of the curse was that human relationships would become so damaged that men would seek to subjugate their wives and they would struggle with conflict in their relationships. And if Adam and Eve's marital estrangement did not make the point strongly enough – that disobedience causes more tragedy when their elder son murders the younger. We live in a world that is still infected by the fall and where family life is still a battle zone. We may not experience our children murdering each other, but there are plenty of family breakdowns around us both in marriage and in parenthood. As Christians, we need to watch out for two main dangers.

Firstly, we can give family the wrong place in our lives by putting it above our worship for God, not as part of it. Some singles may face this temptation as they struggle with making sure that a longing for children or a partner does not become a barrier in their worship of God. Some husbands and wives may face this temptation as they struggle with making sure that their affection for each other does not turn into idolisation. Some parents may face this temptation as they have to make sure that they do not worship their children, by being overprotective or by trying to live out their own dreams through them. If we are not careful, we can end up making our families the center of our universe, which is not only unhealthy for them, it is unhealthy for us and our relationship with our Father in heaven.

Abraham loved his son. Isaac was born to him when he was very old: the Bible says that "Abraham was as good as dead" (Rom. 4). Isaac was Abraham's first legitimate child with his wife Sarah. They had been promised him by God and finally, after twenty-five years of waiting, Isaac arrived. Abraham was in a dangerous position. He treasured his only son, promised by God. But would he put his love for Isaac above his love for God? God asked Abraham to sacrifice his only son on Mount Moriah and Abraham passed the test. As Abraham lifted the knife to slay his son, no one could doubt that his allegiance was primarily to God, and that his trust in God and his promises was absolute.

God was teaching Abraham something that Jesus reiterated for all disciples. We are to love God more than we love our families. We are to obey God above our family. Jesus said: "If anyone comes to me and does not hate his father and mother, his wife and children, his brothers and sisters – yes, even his own life – he cannot be my disciple. And anyone who does not carry his cross and follow me cannot be my disciple" (Luke 14:26-27).

Jesus did not come to abolish the Old Testament Law but to fulfill it, so we must not interpret these verses in a way that is at odds with both the command to honor father and mother and the command to love our neighbor as ourself. Jesus himself prohibited hatred and demonstrated incredible care for his mother even making sure she would be taken care of, while he was gasping for breath on the cross.

But in the New Testament the word "hate" can be a comparative word meaning to love less. Jesus is arguing that the priority in our lives must be to put God above all other responsibilities that we have. God comes first: he is the one we are seeking to please. If ever there is a choice between obeying a relative or obeying God, God takes precedence. God is to be the center of our lives.

Care of elderly relatives, concern for our children's education and welfare, and support for an unconverted spouse are all vitally important and must be undertaken with the utmost diligence. However, they are not the things we live for. We serve God primarily, and his call on our lives must come above these family matters. They should not prevent us from worshipping God or serving him in the places he sends us.

Family matters

Secondly, it is possible to fall into the opposite trap, and to push the family so far from the center of our lives that it becomes peripheral. Some of us do that through following our own personal interests or pursuing ambition or financial security. It is all too easy to take advantage of the government aided childcare schemes in order to earn enough for a fantastic holiday – with a kids' club and babysitting service provided. It is often more relaxing and rewarding to spend time in the office than in the family living room. It is perhaps convenient to think that our grandparents are being well looked after in their nursing homes as we work hard at looking after ourselves.

It is also possible to get so caught up in the business of serving God that we neglect our families. We may feel we deserve a pat on the back for all we do in the church – repairing the building, cleaning, youth work, coffee rotas, babysitting rotas, prayer meetings, Bible study meetings and program planning meetings. The Bible has this to say.

> But if a widow has children or grandchildren, these should learn first of all to put their religion into practice by caring for their own family and so repaying their parents and grandparents, for this is pleasing to God ... If anyone does not provide for his relatives, and especially for his immediate family, he has denied the faith and is worse than an unbeliever (1 Tim. 5:4,8).

Paul is clear in his teaching to Timothy and the church he was leading that we are called to care for our families and implies that unbelievers are sometimes better than us at understanding the duty involved. Caring for our relatives is built into human consciousness, and is to be the minimum acceptable standard for Christians. We cannot excuse ourselves with busyness, either at work or in the church.

Christians do not have a spiritual amnesty that means that normal rules of society and family life do not apply to them, but rather we are to show the world that we are being transformed by the grace of God as we relate with one another. How can we credibly talk to others about the love of God, if we are unable to show even basic human love to our families?

We live in a society that is becoming more and more individualistic. Western culture focuses more on rights than on duty and encourages the individual to aim at self-fulfilment. This teaches that whatever is helpful to reach that goal is good and whatever impedes self-fulfilment is bad, leaving duty as an old-fashioned and restrictive concept. Talking to people from non-western cultures, it is difficult to explain that family mealtimes are a rare event or to describe (let alone justify) the concept of an "old people's home". Caring for our parents and relatives, budgeting for the needs of our dependants and participating in family life is nevertheless basic discipleship.

But reinstating our duty to our families is not enough in and of itself. Caring for our families is more than doing the right thing. We have been designed to bring God pleasure through the way that we care for our families. Changing nappies, cooking dinners, pouring coffees, going to Sports Days, giving lifts, hospital visiting, researching mobility aids, arranging haircuts, cutting nails, spending time talking and listening to our families is all honoring to God. This can bring a smile to God's face as much as singing tunefully on a Sunday morning or delivering leaflets for your church. And it teaches us the practice of godliness as our families are the training ground for our discipleship.

We need to ask ourselves if we have begun to idolise our family, putting all our time or effort into pleasing or serving one or more particular member. Does our care routine mean we have no time to pray? Does our marriage lead to others feeling excluded? Do our hopes and plans for the future rely on the well-being of our family? We also need to check if we have shirked family responsibility. Do we care for our children – giving them the time and the support they need? Do we care for our parents – when they are lonely, sick or dying? Are we around enough at those family moments – meal-times, holidays, when the exam results come out, when the hospital results come back, for anniversaries and birthdays?

Jesus once called a man to follow him. The man, who was caring for his aging father, replied "First let me go and bury my father" (Luke 9:60). This prospective disciple was asking Jesus if he could put off discipleship until he was relieved of responsibility for his father and the funeral was behind him. This seemed like a legitimate request but Jesus knows when people are using caring for their families as an excuse to disobey his call on their lives to radical discipleship. Jesus also knows when we are using God's call on our lives to radical discipleship to disobey God's command to care for our families. To one man Jesus says "Come and follow me, leave your family." To another man, who was begging to follow him, Jesus says "Return home and tell how much God has done for you" (Luke 8:39).

There is a creative tension between these two extremes of idolatry and irresponsibility. We are to reject all family calls on us in order to follow God, and in following God we are to worship him by showing godly love and care to the world around us, beginning with our family. We must be careful not to sacrifice our family lives at the altar of the service of God, but we must also be careful not to sacrifice the service of God on the altar of the family.

Happy families

I had a friend at school who was difficult to complain to. No matter what I said, his instant reply was, "You think that's bad. I…" If I had been teased, he had been beaten up; if I was nervous about an exam, he had already failed. If I had toothache, he had a broken limb. If I had a broken limb, he had an incurable disease and so it went on. Despite being somewhat annoying, it did help me get things in perspective. My Dad often quoted a proverb his father had taught him: "I thought I was poor because I had no shoes but then I met a man who had no feet." He was also trying to help me keep things in perspective whenever I faced problems. So was my friend Vova, who taught me the Russian proverb: "Things are never so bad, that they can't get even worse."

There is some comfort, or at least a challenge to be more contented and less complaining, in knowing that we are better off than others, but what is even more comforting is God's insistence of taking the weakest, most dysfunctional families and making them examples of his grace. We all fall into one or both of the traps we have discussed above, and most families, as you get to know them, are uniquely dysfunctional somewhere. We have already looked back at the mess our first ancestors made of family life, and reading on in our spiritual family tree in the Bible helps us to know that no matter how mixed up our families are, they can be the arena for God to show his sovereign grace.

Abraham's grandson Jacob is a prime example. He did not get on with his brother Esau at all, his father Isaac favored his brother, and his mother favored him. So Jacob tricked his brother, who happened to favor his stomach, and then wanted to kill Jacob. Jacob fled for his life and never saw his mother or father again. He fell in love and worked seven years to win his dream girl's hand in marriage but woke up after the wedding day with a hangover and the wrong wife. A bad day? Jacob was having a bad life. He worked for another seven years and married the woman of his dreams. So did he live happily ever after? No way. There began a terrible feudal struggle between his wives, who were also sisters, which was taken out on the naming of the children. I don't know how you chose or would choose what you call your children, but I hope it is not in the fashion of Leah and Rachel. A name like "Surely my husband will love me now" was not going to foster family stability. Rachel was so jealous of her sister that she felt suicidal, and came up with a plan to get the maidservants involved. Both sides could play at that game and further children were named as part of the manipulation. In the end twelve sons were born into this battle to be loved and they began their own tale of jealousy, treachery, murder plots, sexual improprieties and lies. But these sons of the strange dysfunctional line of Jacob were not just any old sons. They were the twelve boys that God chose to be the founding fathers of the nation of Israel. God turned an incredibly dysfunctional family into the family that would be called his people and eventually bring God's own Son into the world.

Throughout the Bible, God deliberately chooses to show his love and grace to broken families. This gives us great encouragement because, whatever the state of our families, God can use them to show his love. In fact it seems that God delights in turning around messed-up lives in order to show that his ends are achieved not by our own efforts but his grace. God delights in using the weak to shame the strong.

Often we try and keep up an image about our families; we feel we have to look as if everything is going well, ticking along without any of those problems that characters in soap operas face. Of course soap operas are so popular exactly because the characters face the same dilemmas we do. Even cartoons can come frighteningly close to the truth. Ned Flanders of *The Simpsons* is a caricature Christian neighbor to Homer Simpson, and wants everyone to think his family is "okily-dokily" perfect even as he faces temptation, feuding neighbours, a house fire, emotional breakdown and bereavement.

Because we wrongly assume that Christians living in the grace of God can handle all of life's problems without a struggle, we are forced to put up a façade that says we have no problems. The Bible is clear that we should not do that. The Bible is full of faulty people being used by a faultless God. It tells of families that should have fallen apart being held together by the love of God; not publicly humiliated but publicly humbled to prove God's ability to handle life's problems.

We have all seen the adverts for anti-dandruff shampoo on television. They are effective because they begin with someone who has a terribly itchy, flaky scalp. The worse the 'before picture' is, the better their 'after picture' will look. We are wowed by the dramatic transformation a particular brand can make and we all rush out to buy it. As Christians, we are in the process of being transformed by the power of God. God takes broken dysfunctional families and shows the world that he is in control. If the world doesn't see the before picture of our brokenness, then it can't see the after picture of our healing. Contrary to all our instincts, our private family life needs to be out in the open, in public, just as the families of Jacob, Moses, Ruth, David, Job and Jesus himself were. There need be no shame in the problems we face: toddlers with tantrums, out-of-control teenagers, prodigal sons, marriage difficulties, nagging parents, prosecution, debt, depression or death. God wants our family lives to be demonstrations of his character, as he helps us to work hard at holding our families together against the odds.

Family breeds contempt?

There is a place for privacy in family life, but it is not to enable us to compete with our neighbors for the better life, but in order that we might see ourselves as we really are. However much we try to be ourselves at work or at church, our guard is really only down with our families. Like a CCTV camera that catches us unawares and reveals what we are up to when no one else is looking, so families are the environments that show us our true colors. And we probably don't always like what we see. Our fuses are shorter with our families, our voices louder in argument, our words sharper, our gazes more cutting; we are grumpier, moodier and more demanding. Families see us at our worst – when we are tired and ill and when we are having a rough time. And so God in his wisdom gives us families to reveal our faults, to support us in our struggles, and to encourage us to become more Christ-like. Family life is the testing ground of Christian discipleship and the coalface of God's grace in our lives. We must learn to be grateful for this.

I never realised how selfish I was until I got married. All of a sudden I was aware that every decision I had ever made was by myself and for myself. How late to stay out, which take-away to visit, or how loud to play my music were choices I could no longer make simply to please myself. As I learned to compromise in these areas to please my wife, and as she compromised to please me, we learned together about becoming less selfish and more Christ-like.

We may be especially conscious of our need for godliness if we are in families that include people who are not believers. Our unbelieving husbands, parents or children are watching to see if our faith is merely a human invention. The Bible counsels us not to try and nag our family into the kingdom of God, but to mostly win them over without words (1 Pet. 3:1-2). This is an incredibly hard calling and the church has to do all that it can to support those in these circumstances. God calls our lives to be a living demonstration of the gospel. This is not a call to sinless perfectionism, but a call to radical gospel living that demonstrates God's purity and our awe at the greatness of God. This involves being open with our family members about the struggles we face as a Christian, the need to keep on going back to God for his empowering by his Spirit and fresh forgiveness for our daily sins. Through this our lives become the persuasive force of the gospel for those nearest and dearest to us.

All Christians need to learn to accept God's help and discipleship in our family lives. In Titus and 1 Timothy we are given lists of leadership qualities and high up comes care for the family. "He must handle his own affairs well, attentive to his own children and having their respect. For if someone is unable to handle his own affairs, how can he take care of God's church?" (1 Tim. 3:4-5 *The Message*).

When Bill Clinton's affair with Monica Lewinsky became the top news story around the world, the discussion concluded that Clinton's ability to lead the nation, his economic policies and his grasp of the political landscape were not impaired by his domestic problems. Conversely, the Bible teaches that if leaders cannot be faithful to their families then they will not be faithful in church leadership. Family life is the proving ground, not only for our own godliness but also for potential church leadership, because loving a family teaches us the necessary skills and refines and demonstrates our true characters.

Adopted family

The story goes that a little girl was being picked on at school because her classmates discovered that she was adopted. The girl turned to her taunters and had the last word: "At least my family chose me." God uses the picture of adoption to describe how people like you and me could be accepted into God's family. God knew us, knew exactly what we were like with all of our sins and flaws, and yet he chose to welcome us into his family.

Friends of mine who adopted an orphan from China waited many months, filled in endless amounts of paperwork and paid out thousands of pounds to adopt their beautiful baby daughter, a girl who will always know how precious she is to her new parents because of the lengths they went to in order to make her part of the family. The cost of our adoption into God's family was nothing less than the death of his only Son on the cross. God's Son became estranged from the Father in order that we could be welcomed into the family. Jesus carried the shame of all of our sin and was rejected by his Father in order that we could be accepted as children of God. For Jesus to cry, "My God, my God, why have you forsaken me?" (Matt. 27:46) was the most terrifying moment of the crucifixion, as the perfect family became a broken family because of our sin. And so Jesus died isolated, alone and estranged from his dearly loved Father. But God vindicated Jesus' life and death by raising him up from the grave, demonstrating to the world that Jesus was the true Son of God. If we must never take our earthly families for granted, how much more should we be eternally grateful for being part of God's family.

Family likeness

An enterprising Scotsman in the eighteenth century decided it would be a good idea to connect each type of tartan with the different clans. There was no such practice, but it was a great business idea. Belonging to a family, tracing our family trees, discovering people in our ancestry and finding a way to mark the connection is one of our most basic instincts. Note how many genealogies there are all through the Bible. We have a trademark family connection to God – our character. We are to be like him, as we love, as we care, as we discipline, as we make decisions, and as we face struggles. Just like relatives pore over a newborn baby in an effort to spot the family resemblances, so people rightly come looking for the family likeness in us as Christians. They are looking for godliness and they have every right to expect it. I have inherited things from my earthly parents, certain dispositions due to both nurture and nature, and as a Christian I now have a new nature that can nurture family traits that will bring glory to God.

One of God's primary tasks is bringing peace; peace between God and us and peace between human beings. Jesus said, "Blessed are the peacemakers for they will be called the sons of God" (Matt. 5:9). People will recognise our family likeness if we seek peace. What a high calling for us in our families. In a society that believes separation is the best cure for conflict, we should model God's likeness and try to bring peace. This could start with a very simple step such as pledging to take the initiative in asking for forgiveness and reconciliation when things go wrong or by resolving to "never let the sun go down on our anger."

Extended family

God has chosen the picture of family to describe his own being, his own expectations of us, and his own relationship with us. But it doesn't stop there.

When one of my (other very distant) relatives and her husband adopted three sisters, they not only gave the girls a new surname, they also invited and helped them to choose new first names for themselves. They gained a whole new identity, and now not only had new parents to get to know, but also new grandparents, cousins, uncles and aunts. When we are adopted into God's family, we do not only gain a new identity as a child of God, we also gain brothers and sisters around the world. God chooses to use the picture of family for the church because Christianity is all about relationships. We are called to love the Lord our God and to love our neighbor as ourselves. Paul makes this practical: "Do not rebuke an older man harshly, but exhort him as if he were your father. Treat younger men as brothers, older women as mothers, and younger women as sisters, with absolute purity" (1 Tim. 5:1-2).

We must see the church as our new family and care for them as we care for our own households. Nobody should be without a family. The widows, the orphans, the singles in our church should be especially cared for as the Bible is shot through with God's special concern for those who have no natural families and we should reflect that. King David, great-great-grandson of Ruth, who was "redeemed" by Boaz into his family, described God as the defender of the vulnerable in the Psalms

Sing to God, sing praise to his name,
extol him who rides on the clouds –
his name is the LORD –
and rejoice before him.
A father to the fatherless, a defender of widows,
is God in his holy dwelling.
God sets the lonely in families,
he leads forth the prisoners with singing;
but the rebellious live in a sun-scorched land

(Ps. 68:4-6).

The great powerful God who rules the heavens is quick to use his power to help the vulnerable. He is a Father to the orphan, and a Carer for the lonely. The church that dares to call itself the body of Christ must be like its head. The church is the place where those without family are welcome. We keep our eyes and hearts open for the vulnerable, we become their family, we look out for their needs, and we care for them as if they were our own flesh and blood.

Re-generation

God always meant for worship to be an inter-generational family thing. As he instructed the Jewish people how to worship, he instigated community and family traditions that would be passed down through the generations. As we learn to appreciate the privilege of being adopted into God's family, we as a church can help protect each other from idolising and sidelining our flesh and blood families. We can do this by passing on the gospel through the generations, and by living out the gospel as we generously and sacrificially care for one another, showing supernatural unconditional love, acceptance and faithfulness. "By this all men will know that you are my disciples" (Jn. 13:35).

Just a minute

Find ways to weave worship of your heavenly Father into the warp and woof of daily family life. Whether you have biological children or not, think about how you can be a spiritual mother or father to younger people in your church family. If possible, get on a rota to help out with the children's program at church, or think about how you can invest time in the lives of younger people.

As you plan your Christmas celebrations, look out for those who have no families – the international students far away from home or those that would be shut in over the vacation.

Consider a scheme where you can adopt a grandmother in the third world by sponsoring them through monthly giving, or support work done to help the frail or needy in your own church community.

Make the most of the time you have with your own parents by looking for ways to express appreciation for the work they put into raising you.

If you have children, bring your faith into everyday conversation. It could start with something as simple as saying grace before meals, by collecting prayer requests before you tuck in, or using bath time as a way to read the Bible to a captive audience.

Be honest with friends about the ups and downs of family life. Ask for support. Go on a marriage enrichment course. Set time aside regularly to spend with your spouse.

Pray regularly for members of your family who do not follow Christ, and ask God to help you as you witness quietly to them.

On the iPod

We Are Family, Sister Sledge (Cotillion, 1979)
He Ain't Heavy, He's My Brother, The Hollies (Parlophone, 1969)
Father God I Wonder, Ian Smale (Kingsway Music, 1984)
Better Together, Jack Johnson (Brushfire/Universal Records, 2005)
How Deep the Father's Love For Us, Stuart Townend (Kingsway Music, 1995)

Off the shelf

Paul Tripp, *Age of Opportunity* (Phillipsburg: P & R Publishing, 1991)
Douglas Coupland, *All Families Are Psychotic* (London: Flamingo, 2001)
Rodney Clapp, *Families At the Crossroads* (Leicester: IVP, 1993)
Jerry Bridges, *Practice of Godliness* (Colorado Springs: NavPress, 1996)
Jung Chang, *Wild Swans* (London: HarperPerennial, 2004)

FUN

PURE PLEASURE

Can leisure bring pleasure to God?

It felt like I was caught in a film that was stuck in slow motion. Mr Jones' physics class had this incredibly ironic way of proving that time was relative. The clock always seemed to grind to a halt, seconds managed to stretch out into hours. Every eye in the class was focussed just above Jones' head on the unnaturally slow minute hand of the class clock. After an eternity the bell would finally sound and it had the same effect as the starting pistol in a one hundred metre sprint as every student in the room tried to be the first to escape out of the door. That lesson lasted longer than the school holidays in my memory. They were always gone before you could blink, and I would be back in Jones' class, staring at the clock with a feeling of déjà vu.

Free time, leisure and pleasure: we long for it, but before we have even begun to enjoy it, it is gone. We all want to know how we can get the most out of our leisure time. But over and above that, how can our leisure bring pleasure to God?

What do we mean by leisure? Functionally leisure is the opposite of work. Work can be defined as that which we do because of obligation, whether we enjoy it or not. This extends our definition of work beyond the career and includes activities such as cleaning the car, mowing the lawn, preparing the flowers for church, collecting our children from sleepovers, preparing a meal or fixing the shower. These are things we know we ought to do; we do them out of a sense of obligation and responsibility. However there are other things we do simply because we want to do them – they bring us pleasure. This is leisure.

Just like my schoolmates waiting to get out of physics class, some Christians await the bell at the end of their shift as though it marks a transition from the work part of the day to the fun part of the day. These people are not going to go

home and take up household responsibilities or family commitments – they will often socialise with friends, and come
home to put their feet up in front of the TV. Caring for elderly parents, helping a neighbor, or volunteering to help
with the youth work at church are responsibilities that they
wish to avoid in their pursuit of leisure.

Alternatively other Christians feel leisure is a waste of
time. These Christians believe so strongly in the ethic of
work, duty and responsibility that they cannot stop working.
Time not spent working feels empty and extravagant. They
often begin to judge other Christians for not pulling their
weight, especially when there is so much to be done. These
Christians sign up for everything that's going on, and are
often motivated for church activities by their own misplaced
sense of guilt.

Somewhere between these two positions is a happy
medium. We have already considered a biblical approach to
work, and in the final chapter we will look at the idea of rest.
But where does leisure fit in? What is the correct approach to
leisure? Let us take a leisurely look at what the Bible says
about enjoying our free time.

A happy God

The definition of leisure as activities done neither to earn
money nor out of obligation can be applied to God. God is
under no obligation to do anything at all, he is completely
free and sovereign. God has no needs and no compulsions.
The Bible says "Our God is in heaven; he does whatever
pleases him" (Ps. 115:3). Our God is a God of pleasure.

This is radically different to the view that most people
have of God. When God appears on the Simpsons, for example, he is portrayed as a white bearded old man with a long
face and a very serious voice. The church too is often guilty

of projecting God as a cosmic spoilsport. Many people out-side of the church have the impression that we worship a frustrated or angry God. They believe that God has the inten-tion of turning us into monks dressed in dark brown, who eat gruel for breakfast, spend twenty hours a day in prayer and walk around feeling somber. For some people pleasure and Christianity are antonyms; polar opposites. Even Christians are likely to hold a picture in their minds of God with a permanent scowl as he fumes at the sin in the world, or of God with a constant flow of tears from his eyes as he weeps for a lost world. Few of us meditate on God's smiling face.

Of course God is Spirit – he does not have a physical body or a physical face. Yet Scripture is replete with language that expresses truth about God by figuratively assigning him physical attributes. Scripture describes God in terms that we can understand. The Bible does describe God as angry (Jer. 10:10). The Bible does describe God as grieving over the rebellion of mankind (Gen. 6:6). But the Bible also describes God as being pleased: a happy God. God enjoys who he is and what he does. God works, not out of obligation, but for the delight in it. God rests to enjoy and appreciate his cre-ation. Pleasure is a divine attribute that God has also passed on to us as people made in his image.

Pleasure gardens

God would have made a cathedral if humanity's chief end was to sing songs and listen to preaching. God would have made a factory if humanity's chief end was to work. But God made paradise because the chief end of humanity was to enjoy God and his creation. Paradise literally means a pleas-ure park. God created a pleasure garden for Adam and Eve that he filled with beautiful things. God was not minimalist, giving only what we needed: nor was he utilitarian, giving only what would be useful. God was holistic and generous, providing a place much better than we could ever appreciate.

When I visit my parents for the day, my Mum packs the freezer ready for a whole week. When we visit for a weekend, the freezer is packed with a month's supply of delicious cooking. She has everything ready – just in case. My mum expresses love through provision. This seems to reflect God's design strategy when he created the earth; prepare abundantly more than is necessary so we can have our pick of the treasures. He packed the earth with exciting things to discover – like gold, diamonds and oil.

God demonstrated aesthetic awareness; he made Eden a beautiful place with trees, wildlife, and winding rivers. God showed an appreciation of taste and texture, by making food tasty for our eating pleasure. God wanted to give us social pleasure and made the first family. God was gracious to humanity, making sexuality for recreation as well as procreation. God went to great lengths to put us in an enjoyable environment. God expresses his love for us by providing for us.

And so we must never doubt that although we were designed to handle responsibility, we were also designed for leisure and that when we are enjoying our time off, we are enjoying what God has created us to do – this can be worship.

I have travelled the road between Macedonia and Albania many times. There is a bend in the road just at the brow of the hill where the panorama opens up over a sapphire blue glimmering lake with sandy beaches and small fishing boats in the foreground and snow-capped mountains in the distance. Every time I go round that corner I pull into the lay-by and take time to enjoy the view and praise its Maker. Then I take out my camera to try and capture the beauty that I failed to catch the previous time I went over that hill.

God gave human beings the ability to appreciate beauty. As we close the curtains on a starry night, or open them on a beautiful sunrise, as we travel, holiday and take walks in the countryside, nature prompts us and inspires us to worship God for his beautiful world.

My dog who traveled with me on that same journey between Albania and Macedonia was also very excited as we pulled over in that lay-by at the top of the hill. He would jump out of the car and relieve himself under an olive tree, before finding a dead rodent or bird to play with. Although God obviously gave animals, or at least the animals I have known, zero appreciation for the wonder of a beautiful view, he did give them an ability to play and have fun. The Bible describes the spring lambs and other creatures "playing" together (Job 40:20). Even the sea monster was formed by God to "frolic" in the ocean (Ps. 104:26). And if God takes delight even in the animals enjoying their leisure, how much more does he delight in the enjoyment of human beings, the pinnacle of creation?

No fun please, we're Christians

Some Christians try to stand against the culture by being as sober as possible. They don't laugh or joke. The philosopher H.L. Mencken once described Puritanism as "the haunting fear that somewhere someone was enjoying themselves." This description was inaccurate, but it does describe some Christians' view of life. We can effectively destroy pleasure in our lives in many ways, but one way is by overworking. It is easy to fall into the trap of turning our work into our god. Running a household is a never-ending cycle of washing, cleaning and ironing that is around us 24 hours a day. DIYers are forever spotting the things that need fixing, because earthly things will inevitably break and wear out. Evangelists find it hard to have a night out at a restaurant without feeling the obligation to win over the waiter for Christ. Office workers pick up their laptops, mobile phones, briefcases and a few papers when they leave the office – surely the pressure will be off if they just do half an hour at home? We need to remember that we were not created only to work.

The idea of actively pursuing something that we enjoy, just for the sake of fun, is hard for some of us to take seriously. Some people talk about leisure as a chance to recharge their batteries, to be refreshed so that they can work again, but that is still making work the primary goal of our lives. Some things God just wants us to enjoy. If work dominates our lives, we are rejecting God's gifts of leisure and pleasure.

Christians throughout the centuries have been good at refusing to take pleasure seriously enough. They had a very low view of pleasure when they banned dancing, theater, and cinema-going. This low view of pleasure often meant rejection of God's good gifts, and focused on micro-ethical issues to the exclusion of God's concern for the bigger picture. The Pharisees were criticised by Jesus for having a similar approach to holiness.

We need to be careful not to be stricter than God. The confusion comes with the definition not of pleasure but of holiness. Holiness means being set apart for God's purposes. Sometimes in the name of religion elaborate systems of prohibitions are created. This often leads to religious leaders losing the plot when it comes to holiness. Take, for example, Paul's critique of the false teachers in his first letter to his close friend Timothy.

"They forbid people to marry and order them to abstain from certain foods, which God created to be received with thanksgiving by those who believe and who know the truth. For everything God created is good, and nothing is to be rejected if it is received with thanksgiving, because it is consecrated by the word of God and prayer" (1 Tim. 4:3-5). Paul's argument is that if our attitude is primarily gratitude to God for his good gifts then the pleasure we derive from them should flow out in a way that is holy and pleasing to God. The Bible has plenty to say about self-control, conscience and responsibility. Yet Paul here is challenging a super-spiritual asceticism that treats God's good gifts of sexuality, relationships, food and enjoyment as morally suspect. It is hard to argue for an ascetic lifestyle when our Savior was accused of being a glutton and a drunkard and criticised for having too much fun with too many inappropriate kinds of people.

These verses are not a blanket endorsement that morally anything goes if you say a quick thank you prayer afterwards. Some people continue this line of reasoning to argue for drug abuse. They say that if God created the marijuana plant, it is there to be enjoyed. Although they are right in saying that there is nothing intrinsically wrong with it, marijuana like tobacco and alcohol can be used in a wrong way. We can also misuse the iron God left in the earth if we turn it into an iron rod and beat each other over the head with it. We must be careful to use God's good gifts in the way he intended.

Paradise lost

God wants us to enjoy his world and to take pleasure in it. But when Adam and Eve mishandled their privileges and sought pleasure without the Provider's permission, it set a pattern of wrong human behavior. Under the devil's guidance, we took the fruit because we wanted pleasure our way, and let our desire for pleasure itself overtake our desire for the pleasure Provider. When we saw that the fruit was "good for food and pleasing to the eye", we did as we pleased and not what pleased God. Pleasure in itself is not wrong, but the devil painted a caricature of God for Eve that lingers to this day. The devil portrayed God as the spoilsport, withholding good things from us. He implied that only he knew where the real fun lay, and people today still think the devil is the source of all the fun in the world and that God is the killjoy. That is the complete reversal of the truth. Jesus taught that he came to bring us life in its fullness, while the devil has come to steal, kill and destroy (John 10:10). Jesus taught that the devil takes his pleasure from destroying us, while God takes pleasure in blessing us.

We live in a culture that rightly values pleasure, but that takes it without the Provider's permission. The culture misrepresents leisure as the ultimate goal of an otherwise meaningless life. There was an advertisement on television showing a man sitting on a bench and a piano falling from a window above him. The grim reaper sits down next to him, but the man is happy, because as his life flashes before him, he remembers sun-kissed beaches, jet skiing, parties and plenty of women. This man's life has been so filled with pleasure he can face death with a smile. Philosophy calls this hedonism – a lust for pleasure at all costs. Our culture says: "If it feels good do it" or "If it makes you happy, it can't be that bad." Most of us make our decisions in life based on what makes us feel good or what brings us enjoyment. The Bible warns us about this when it differentiates "lovers of pleasure" from "lovers of God" (1 Tim. 3:4).

Please yourself

Enjoying our Creator's good creation is supposed to bring us closer to him. I will always remember my two-year-old son eating donuts on a picnic, his eyes opening up as the bag opened, his little tongue licking his lips, his mouth stretching as wide as it would go around the huge feast, and then smiling from ear to ear with sugar, dough and jam all over his face. He did not need to say it, but he managed a sticky "Thank you, Daddy", and that just crowned it. I got immense pleasure watching him enjoy the gift I had given him. His enjoyment and his gratitude together combined to bring us closer as father and son. But there would have been no pleasure, no bonding if my son had stolen the donut. That would have been selfishness and betrayal and would have resulted in my displeasure and his punishment. The whole picnic would have been spoilt.

God our Maker knows us inside out and knows what will bring us genuine enjoyment. But when we seek pleasure on our own terms, the pleasure becomes betrayal and sin. When we do things our way, we let pleasure rule us and pleasure may be a good servant but it is a terrible master. The world seeks its pleasures without reference to God. It wants the pleasure that God has provided but it will not acknowledge God as the Provider. Once pleasure has become our god, we are in real danger.

Pleasure has to fit into a relationship with God and it also has to fit into God's design. Sex is a pure pleasure within a God-seeking marriage. Eating is a pure pleasure within God's command to take care of our bodies. Leisure is pure pleasure within the God-given work/rest balance. Without God in the picture, those good gifts can easily turn into adultery, greed, and selfishness.

Without God in the picture, it is easy to follow the world's example and worship pleasure. We live for pleasure, shirk responsibility and put pleasing ourselves top of our agenda. The Bible has plenty to say to those of us tempted to fall into that trap, such as. "He who loves pleasure will become poor; whoever loves wine and oil will never be rich" (Prov. 21:17).

But these men blaspheme in matters they do not understand. They are like brute beasts, creatures of instinct, born only to be caught and destroyed, and like beasts they too will perish. They will be paid back with harm for the harm they have done. Their idea of pleasure is to carouse in broad daylight. They are blots and blemishes, reveling in their pleasures while they feast with you. With eyes full of adultery, they never stop sinning; they seduce the unstable; they are experts in greed – an accursed brood! (2 Pet. 2:12-14).

Joy to the world

How many festivals did God incorporate into the Jewish diary? How many celebrations and parties are mentioned in the Bible during Jesus' lifetime? God leaves us with no room for doubt that he enjoys parties and that we too should rejoice with our Father in heaven.

There were more useful miracles that Jesus could have done for his opening act; he could have healed someone, fed someone, rescued someone. But Jesus' first public miracle was to make sure a wedding party did not run out of alcohol. Jesus' first miracle was significant as a foretaste both of the Last Supper and also of the great wedding feast at the end of time between Jesus and the Church. But just as important, Jesus' first miracle was significant because it reflected God's pleasure and enjoyment as he interacted with the human race he created.

This did not mean that those who followed Jesus lived a life of non-stop fun, leisure and prosperity – often it meant the opposite, and Jesus was very clear in explaining the cost of discipleship to those who were considering following him. But Jesus' followers certainly had times of enjoyment being in his company. Jesus encouraged us to pray for heaven on earth when he taught his disciples to pray that God's will be done on earth as in heaven. But he did not promise that this prayer would be answered immediately. But neither did Jesus delay all gratification until heaven. Jesus gave people a sample, or a demo version of heaven right here, right now. Jesus improved the quality of people's lives: he satisfied people's hunger and gave them a picnic. He healed a para-lyzed man who jumped for joy. According to the gospels Jesus ruined every funeral that he went to, turning mourn-ing into dancing, wakes into celebrations. As we share Jesus with the world around us, we must be careful not to paint a picture of ease and lifelong parties, but as we see people encounter Jesus, we can expect a new level of enjoyment and fulfilment in their lives.

> "However, do not rejoice that the spirits submit to you, but rejoice that your names are written in heaven." At that time Jesus, full of joy through the Holy Spirit, said, "I praise you, Father, Lord of heaven and earth, because you have hidden these things from the wise and learned, and revealed them to little children. Yes, Father, for this was your good pleasure" (Luke 10:20-21).

God seems to have set up the mathematics of pleasure in such a way that a pleasure shared is a pleasure doubled – or even tripled. In this passage we see the Trinity; Father, Son and Holy Spirit, experiencing pleasure together with the disciples as they do mission. Being a follower of Jesus is to be a part of that mission and also part of the enjoyment of the Trinity. Jesus' ministry, without doubt was hard work and yet it brought him intense pleasure.

It was this pleasure that Jesus was thinking about as he was bearing the sins of the world. When Jesus was dying, he turned and said to the repentant thief on the cross beside him: "Today you will be with me in paradise." We have already seen how paradise originally referred to the Garden of Eden. Now it refers to heaven. Heaven is often described negatively – no more tears, no more mourning, no more pain. Put the other way round, we see that God is preparing a place for us of fun, laughter and enjoyment. We simply get to enjoy God, each other and the perfect new creation, living together in harmony. Heaven will be so good, that it is impossible for the Bible to fully describe it to us. Instead we are given clues, hints and word pictures. There are images of a feast, a party, a wedding, a celebration, a city, singing and dancing. We will finally see God's face – and he will be smiling.

Pleased to meet you

C.S. Lewis describes how in our highest pleasures we often hear an echo of heaven. He explains how God whispers to us in our pleasures. In other words there is a longing in us that no pleasure on earth can fully satisfy. This may help us to understand why, despite feeling overworked, we actually have more leisure time and disposable income than ever before and many people experience boredom on a regular basis. It is because of boredom that many of us switch television channels, switch jobs and even switch marriage partners. There is a longing that no pleasure seems to fully satisfy. The book of Ecclesiastes logically works through the pleasures of this world: food, drink, work and possessions.

"I denied myself nothing my eyes desired; I refused my heart no pleasure. My heart took delight in all my work, and this was the reward for all my labor" (Eccl. 2:10). Although the author concludes that these things bring some satisfaction; without a relationship with God these pleasures are meaningless. Then the author makes his summarising statement

> Then I realized that it is good and proper for a man to eat and drink, and to find satisfaction in his toilsome labor under the sun during the few days of life God has given him – for this is his lot. Moreover, when God gives any man wealth and possessions, and enables him to enjoy them, to accept his lot and be happy in his work – this is a gift of God. He seldom reflects on the days of his life, because God keeps him occupied with gladness of heart (Eccl. 5:18-20).

We cannot truly enjoy life until God has enabled us to do so. Enjoyment as given by God is a great pleasure. Enjoyment as shared with God is the greatest pleasure. Enjoying God is the chief end of humanity, and our chief destiny for those of us who rejoice that our names are written in the Lamb's book of life.

Bored to death

We look around at a bored culture, with many people going to extreme lengths to find some pleasure in life, whether that is through huge investments of cash in faster cars and bigger houses, investment of time escaping to the virtual world of computer games or escaping from life through mind-altering drugs. People are looking in vain for pleasure. The clearest expression of God's pleasure is given in the three stories of lost things. God is described as being like a shepherd who has found a lost sheep and rejoices; like a woman who has found a precious missing piece of jewelry and puts on a party to celebrate the find and finally like a grieving father who has received his son back from the dead. If we know that this brings unimaginable pleasure to God, how can it not be a central part of the Christian life to do all that we can to join God's mission and help bring lost children, who are bored to death, back to their heavenly Father?

Just a minute

Put dates in your diary where you can review your work/leisure balance. If you have a leisure deficit, find ways to cut down at work, try out a new sport, club, or activity. Ask God to give you friends in these new activities that you could share something of the gospel with. Build space into each day to appreciate God's creation – through walking to the shops or taking a plant into work to take care of, or by setting your desktop background to an inspiring scene of nature. Throw a party or arrange a picnic. Put on some music to inspire you to sing and dance when you are at home. Deliberately reflect on the enjoyment you get from being with your husband or wife, boyfriend or girlfriend, children or family members.

If the work/leisure balance has swung too far over on the leisure side, you might chose to restrict the number of hours you spend on computer games, or tinkering in the garage, or the number of TV shows you watch, perfecting the garden or out on the golf course. Maybe it's time to take on a responsibility at church. Discover the joy of service as you bring joy into the lives of those living in poverty or despair.

As you enjoy yourself, thank God for his provision to you. As you sing and dance, smile and laugh, anticipate the joy of heaven.

On the iPod

Joy To the World, Isaac Watts (1719)
That's Entertainment, The Jam (Polydor Records: 1980)
Have a Nice Day, Stereophonics (V2 Records: 2001)
Sitting On the Dock of the Bay, Otis Redding (Volt Records: 1968)
Mourning Into Dancing, Tommy Walker (Integrity Music: 1991)

Off the shelf

John Piper, *The Pleasures of God* (Portland: Multnomah, 2001)
Richard Winter, *Still Bored In a Culture of Entertainment* (Downers Grove: IVP, 2002)
Neil Postman, *Amusing Ourselves To Death* (London: Penguin 2006)
Nick Pollard and Steve Couch, *Get More like Jesus While Watching TV* (Milton Keynes: Authentic Media, 2006)
Alister McGrath, *A Brief History of Heaven* (Oxford: Blackwells, 2003)

EXERCISE

FIT FOR THE KING

Peak performance

A new you in a week. Kick-start your diet. Improve your sports performance. Drop a dress size. Boost your athletic ability. Firm up those bums and tums. Stop gray hair today. New guaranteed effective weight loss diet. Ads like these always make us sit up and take notice. Most of us feel too fat or too thin, too lazy or out of condition. And if diet and exercise won't achieve our ideal look, then the cosmetic surgeon offers to do to it all for us in our sleep.

It is not hard to notice how body conscious our culture has become. Our media presents us constantly not only with advertisements, but with thin girls and muscular men who work out each day in the gym. Even some of our sports stars become famous through their looks, rather than necessarily their talent. One of the largest growth industries is men's cosmetics. Gyms are opening up all over the place. Injecting rat poison into our faces has become a part of life in the cities. Models have been superseded by supermodels.

Whereas our pin-ups come and go, our society has been influenced by one picture of womanhood that we are introduced to in our infancy and that has been around for decades. *The Guardian* newspaper once called her the "synthetic mass-produced godmother of female body dysmorphia."[1] Barbie is anatomically impossible, her neck and her waist are the same size, and her chest is so large she would probably fall over if she could stand up at all. Yet this malformed image of bodily perfection has to take some responsibility for the growth in teenage girls in bulimia and anorexia.

At the other extreme, obesity is also on the increase. This provides plenty of fuel for our comedians. They may have wised up and steered away from racist jokes, but there is no such relief for those of us who are overweight. Yet this is no laughing matter. Diabetes is on the increase and childhood obesity is out of control due to fast food becoming an everyday diet, hours spent in front of the computer, television and Nintendo screens, and the parental door-to-door taxi-service. Life expectancy is being reduced significantly as eating and exercising habits are formed in childhood and are hard to reprogram later in life.

In the face of this overwhelming media bombardment of body image, role models, advice and advertisements, Christians need to think through what they believe and why. We need to face up to the biblical portrait of the body, in order to understand where caring for our bodies and exercise should fit into our daily worship lifestyle.

Body and soul

When God made the first human beings, he made them out of mud. In fact the name "Adam" is a play on the word "ground" in Hebrew. In English, Adam and Eve today might have been called Bert and Girt from the Dirt. These are our predecessors. Like them, our bodies are made up of the same chemicals that make up the rest of the world. They are chemicals that would cost only a few pounds to buy from a shop. This should fundamentally give us a humble self-image.

But God the maker of the Universe, took his newly formed person, and gave him the kiss of life, breathing existence into him. This is an amazing picture of God the Almighty, getting his hands dirty to form us from earth and then drawing closer still to us to give us life. This brings a spiritual dimension to our lowly bodies. When we consider that our bodies are designed by God, temples for the Holy Spirit (1 Cor. 6:9), created before the fall and pronounced very good, we see ourselves in a new perspective. If I were lent my friend's brand new car, I would be extra careful how I drove it; I wouldn't dare take it off road or eat my fish and chips in it and I would certainly make doubly sure that I put the right kind of fuel in it. God has given us our bodies; how much more seriously should we take our responsibility to appreciate them and take care of them

Typically, when my wife goes to get her hair cut, she spends around forty-five minutes with her hairdresser, who not only washes and cuts her hair but spends time sculpting each strand and fixing it in place with the latest technique or gel. She pays her compliments to the artistry, pays her money and nips straight home – to wash and dry it again, embarrassed about that "wash and set" look. She then spends the rest of the day hiding at the back of the house, because she knows her hairdresser always walks past our house on his way home, and she never wants him to feel offended.

When God originally created man and woman, they were naked and there was no shame, we are told. Every part of our bodies was created by a master Craftsman and nothing needed to be hidden or kept private. Adam and Eve felt no shame about the birthday suits God had tailored for them. But then, instead of saying "Yes" to God and "No" to their bodies as they looked at the forbidden fruit, they said "No" to God and "Yes" to their bodies. And God's punishment fell on them. Nothing physical happened to them immediately, but their minds were changed in an instant. They felt shame, they became critical of their own bodies, they realised they were naked, and their instinct was to hide. There was exposure, embarrassment, insecurity, and vulnerability.

These feelings have been passed down through the generations as a consequence of our rebellion against God. Our security system has broken down. When we walk into the gym, we notice the other bodies on the machines, and we surreptitiously check out how we measure up. Going to the beach, the park, a party or the swimming pool can all be overshadowed by a vulnerability based purely on our physical appearance. Taken to an extreme, this vulnerability can lead to eating disorders. For most of us it leads to a self-conscious fear that we will not be respected or loved.

Along with shame came another consequence of Adam and Eve's rebellion – pain. They felt no pain in the Garden of Eden, but after the fall, there was pain in childbirth and toil in work. Here originated aches and pains, arthritis, congenital diseases, cancers and disabilities. And most severely our bodily existence became finite – from dust we were made and to dust we will return. Our bodies will age and wear out, and eventually die and decay. We may fight against this process but it is ultimately a losing battle.

But this losing battle against physical death does not mean that we should not care for our bodies properly in the meantime. God showed us that he had not given up on humankind's bodies in the immediate aftermath of the fall. Although the result of eating the fruit of the tree of the knowledge of good and evil was death, human beings were not executed immediately, nor were they the first things to die as recorded in Genesis. God took pity on them, and killed some of his animals in order to provide coverings for Adam and Eve's bodies. Because of our shame, death was transferred. In our shame, God reached out to us, reaffirming his love and compassion for his disobedient children.

There is a hint here of the covenant God would later establish with the sacrificial system in the Old Testament, where an animal would be ritually slaughtered, symbolising the removal of sins. There is also a hint right here in the beginning of the Old Testament of the perfect Lamb, Jesus, who takes away the sin of the world. As Jesus died naked on the cross, with soldiers casting lots for his clothes, he covered over the shame of our sinfulness in front of a holy God, taking our place as a substitute in order to clothe us in righteousness.,

We learn from the first few pages of the Bible that our bodies were created perfect, and that after the fall, God took care of our broken bodies as well as our alienated spirits. The Old Testament is full of reiterations of this fact. God provided a covenant and chosen spokesmen to lead his people spiritually, but we see him time and again providing basic human bodily needs – food, water and clothing – to the whole community of the people of Israel as they walked through the wilderness, or to the Egyptian people under the leadership of Joseph, and even to seemingly insignificant individuals such as Hagar a maidservant, the widow of Zarephath and Ruth the refugee.

God's provision of our basic physical needs is reinforced in the New Testament as Jesus teaches us not to put our concerns for these things above our worship of God.

> And why do you worry about clothes? See how the lilies of the field grow. They do not labor or spin. Yet I tell you that not even Solomon in all his splendor was dressed like one of these. If that is how God clothes the grass of the field, which is here today and tomorrow is thrown into the fire, will he not much more clothe you, O you of little faith? So do not worry, saying, 'What shall we eat?' or 'What shall we drink?' or 'What shall we wear?' For the pagans run after all these things, and your heavenly Father knows that you need them. But seek first his kingdom and his righteousness, and all these things will be given to you as well
>
> (Matt. 6:28-33).

The Bible teaches us that since God created our bodies and takes care of them, then we should take care of them as well – both our own, and those around us. We should have a self-image that is humble, bearing in mind our lowly origins, and we should also marvel at our high calling, bearing the image of God and being spiritually alive through his breath of life in us. We should accept God's provision of covering for our shame, and we should trust him to provide daily for our needs.

High impact

Not only did God create us embodied, stooping to care for us in our permanent and dependent need, he also undertook the unimaginable leap to become embodied himself and live on earth as one of us. We often take this for granted or fail to grasp the lengths God went for us. The God who made the heavens and earth, the God who is Spirit and everywhere present, willingly took on the limitations and the appetites of a body. He experienced life from our point of view. Jesus experienced the growing pains of childhood and became a man. He went through hunger, thirst, tiredness and physical torture.

The Bible is very sparing in its physical descriptions of people. We know that Esau was hairy, Bathsheba was beautiful and Samson had long hair. We also know Eli was fat, Zacchaeus was short and Goliath was huge. These descriptions are minimal – nothing compared to descriptions you find in novels these days. The Bible doesn't describe any of Jesus' features in this way. Nowhere in the New Testament are we told Jesus' height, weight, stature, eye color, or hairstyle; these things are obviously not significant. The only significant physical description we get in the gospels is that Jesus had scars in his hands, feet and side after the resurrection.

The closest thing we get to a physical description of Jesus elsewhere is found in the book of Isaiah: "He grew up before him like a tender shoot, and like a root out of dry ground. He had no beauty or majesty to attract us to him, nothing in his appearance that we should desire him" (Isa. 53:2). This description in the middle of the prophecy about the life and death of Jesus implies that the most perfect person to walk the face of this planet was physically unattractive and unappealing. This teaches us to get things in perspective. How can we be ashamed of our bodies if Jesus wasn't ashamed of his?

Jesus' incarnation tells us that our body is nothing to be ashamed of. Jesus' actions tell us that he was concerned for the whole person: Jesus touched the rotting bodies of the lepers, he healed a woman with a haemorrhage, he restored sight to the blind, he fed the five thousand. He also commanded us to follow in his footsteps and care for the needs of the poor (Matt. 25:31-46).

Jesus' parable of the Good Samaritan challenges those of us who downplay the Christian's responsibility to care for physical needs. A man beaten and left for dead by robbers is ignored by a priest and a Levite. Neither of them felt it was their job to care for this man; after all they were spiritual leaders. Jesus tells us to emulate the Samaritan who stops and, at risk to himself, helps the man. Our discipleship and our worship involve caring for both bodies and souls – our own and those of others.

No pain, no gain

When Jesus was born, he showed us that an unappealing and needy human body was not too lowly for the Son of God. When Jesus was alive, he showed us what it was to care for other people's bodies as we bring a taste of God's future into the world today. But ultimately Jesus showed us how we should use our bodies for him. Jesus' body was broken for us, so that we could escape punishment and be healed and made whole. Jesus' body was broken for us, which we are visibly reminded of each time we share in communion. Jesus' body broken for us through death on the cross was the ultimate way in which he used his body for the glory of God. Jesus' use of his body shows us how we should use our bodies.

"We always carry around in our body the death of Jesus, so that the life of Jesus may also be revealed in our body. For we who are alive are always being given over to death for Jesus' sake, so that his life may be revealed in our mortal body" (2 Cor. 4:10-11). Paul teaches that our bodies are to be like Jesus' body. Paul is not talking here about stigmata – supernatural scars that suppos-edly develop on hands and feet as we become more Christlike. Paul had his own scars from being beaten and tortured and it is these wounds, acquired because of his testimony for Christ, that reveal the life of Christ in the world today. Paul was not ashamed of them – far from it – he counted physical suffering to be part and parcel of his discipleship as he took up his cross to follow his Lord.

J. Oswald Chambers tells the story of a missionary in India who traveled through the villages sharing the gospel. After a long day on the road and a particularly discouraging visit to one village that had rejected him and his message out-right, he sat under a tree at the edge of the village and fell asleep. When he woke up, he was surrounded by the whole village who was gathered around him asking to hear his message. What had changed them was seeing the mission-ary's blistered feet as he lay sleeping. They realised how much he had been willing to suffer to bring the message to them, and so were willing to give him a hearing.[2]

When people realise that we are willing to suffer even physically and still preach our message of salvation, they will see Jesus' life and death worked out in us. We should not be ashamed of or careless with our bodies as they are the vehi-cles God has chosen to pass on the baton of the gospel. We should not be overprotective of our bodies as we give our-selves in service to God.

Working out our salvation

"For physical training is of some value, but godliness has value for all things, holding promise for both the present life and the life to come" (1 Tim. 4:8). Most of us look after our bodies very satisfactorily – we eat and drink and wash regularly. We count our calories, take our vitamins and visit the doctor when we succumb to ill health. We join a gym or find other ways to exercise. But many of us do not put the same time and effort into our godliness. Paul says while we work out our bodies, we must also be working out our salvation. If we are prepared to sweat over looking after our bodies, which will ultimately wear out, how much more in fact should we be prepared to sweat over looking after our souls which will last an eternity.

This book has tried to show us how our preconceptions of worshipping God need to be transformed from occasional bursts to a permanent practice that infuses all our daily activities with praise. Taking care of our bodies is a strong parallel. Whether we are working, sleeping, or chatting with our family, we can be feeding, resting and exercising our bodies at the same time. As we visit the water cooler, bathroom or snack machine, as we make a cup of coffee or eat our lunch, we can consciously take care both of our bodies and our souls.

Exercising self-control

"Therefore I do not run like a man running aimlessly; I do not fight like a man beating the air. No, I beat my body and make it my slave so that after I have preached to others, I myself will not be disqualified for the prize" (1. Cor. 9:26-27). Paul is also concerned that sometimes physical needs seem to fight with our spiritual needs. This reminds us of where we started in this chapter with Adam and Eve's first sin. We need to ensure that we take every precaution to prevent our body dictating how we should live. Rather it is we who should dictate to our bodies how we should live.

Those of us who have struggled with addictions understand this battle to make our physical bodies obey us, rather than the other way round. Even those of us who have failed to keep a diet will have some idea of these tensions. Jesus' teaching went much further. In the context of adultery, he taught that if what we see causes us to sin, it is better to lose our eyesight than be enslaved to the visual temptations all around us. If we are tempted to reach out for something we should not have, it is better to cut off our hand than sinfully acquire what is not ours. Obviously Jesus is not advocating literal personal dismemberment; he is using strong language to ram the point home. Our bodies, as temples designed by God, need to be controlled so they do not prevent us from worshipping God wholeheartedly.

Body-building

Many sports need us to learn to work together as a team and worshipping God wholeheartedly is not just an individualistic thing. Paul wants us to see ourselves as included in the world-wide church. Paul's teaching of Christians as a worshipping community is based upon the concept of body, working together and interdependent (1 Cor. 12).

The body of God's people is being prepared for God's Son to be his Bride. Many brides-to-be go on a fitness drive in the run up to their wedding, to ensure they fit the dress and look beautiful on the big day. How much more should we, as Christ's Bride, be working hard to get into shape, ready and worthy for our ultimate calling?

We work out because we are responsible for taking care of the bodies God has given us. We work out physically and spiritually. We are prepared to suffer physically for the sake of Christ and for the benefit of others and we are prepared to suffer physically for the sake of holiness. And in our suffering we look forward to heaven. Heaven is where we will be united with Christians from the world over as one body. Heaven is also where God has promised each of us a new body. That body will be better than our previous body; it will be a body that will never wear out, tire or feel pain, a body that will be useful for eternal life (1 Cor. 15:50-54).

Just a minute

As you go to the gym, thank God for your health, and use the time to pray, memorise Scripture or befriend other gym users. If you do not use a gym, check with your doctor how you can exercise effectively. Borrow a pedometer for a week and aim at 10,000 steps a day. Build up your exercise routine by five minutes a week. Get off a stop early on the bus so that you get more time to walk and talk with God.

Decide not to take health for granted and take a look at what you are eating and drinking. Cut back anything that is harmful to your physical or spiritual health.

Use the health in your body to help those too weak to care for themselves. Give up your seat on the tube. Offer to collect prescriptions or groceries for your elderly neighbors.

When you feel ashamed of yourself in the mirror, or envious of bodies on advertisements, remind yourself that you are fearfully and wonderfully made, and thank God for the body he has given you.

When you feel tired or ill, take time to meditate on heaven and look forward to your new body.

On the iPod

Ain't Got No, I Got Life . . ., Nina Simone and Groovefinder
    (BMG: 2006)
Keep Young and Beautiful, Annie Lennox (RCA: 1992)
Keep On Running, Spencer Davis Gr. (Platinum Music: 1966)
Facing A Task Unfinished, Frank Houghton (Overseas
    Missionary Fellowship, 1930)
I Reach Up High, Judy Bailey (Day Break Music: 1993)

Off the shelf

Alan Sillitoe, *The Loneliness of the Long-distance Runner*
    (London: Flamingo, 1993)
Jonathan Edwards, *A Time To Jump* (London: Harper
    Collins, 2001)
Peter Lupson, *Thank God For Football* (London: Azure,
    2006)
Andrew Perriman, *Faith, Health and Prosperity* (Milton
    Keynes: Paternoster, 2003)

Notes

[1] Barbara Ellen in *The Observer*, Sunday, May 5, 2002.
[2] John Piper, *Let the Nations be Glad* (Leicester, IVP, 1994), p.93.

SLEEP

THE REST OF YOUR LIFE

Sleeptalk

Sleep is a subject dear to my heart. As a teenager and as a student, my favorite place was curled up under the duvet. Marriage brought a whole new dimension to activities under the covers, and then our children came along and for five years I had not one uninterrupted night's sleep. Finally my kids slept through the night, but my work has become more demanding and I have indulged in the luxury of a television in the bedroom. This is fatal for my sleep patterns. TV shows, if not essay-marking, keep me up regularly until midnight. Sleep is a precious commodity.

In a work hard, play hard culture, chronic fatigue is taking its toll. We work longer hours, squeeze in a variety of leisure and social interests in the evening, and then come home to watch the late night film every night of the week or challenge the games console to beat us to the next level. We get busier and busier, go to bed later and later and still have to get up the same time in the morning. But even our obsessively busy culture admits – if you burn the candle at both ends, you are bound to get burned or even burned out.

Don't drive tired

In 2002 a man fell asleep at the wheel of his car. He was pulling a trailer, and the car with the trailer careered off the side of the road, down an embankment and onto a train track. An oncoming train was derailed, which also caused a train traveling the opposite direction to crash and derail. Because of one man's tiredness, ten people died and millions was spent on the consequences.

The Selby train crash was not the only disaster in recent times to have been attributed to tiredness. It could well have been a contributing factor to the Chernobyl and Three Mile

Island nuclear disasters, the Challenger space shuttle explosion, the Exxon Valdez oil spill, and the sinking of the ferry the Herald of Free Enterprise.

Tiredness is dangerous. Sleep is important. We never seem to get enough of it although we actually spend a third of our lives in bed. Are we Christians only when we are awake, or also when we are sleeping? If we don't learn how to bring God worship with our rest time then we are short changing God – he deserves our whole lives, not just two thirds. We need to get a biblical picture of sleep to learn how we can worship God with our sleep.

We have already referred several times to the opening chapters of Genesis in this book. This is not coincidental. At the beginning of our life on earth, God introduces all the main facets of human life. Adam woke up. God gave him food and work, family and pleasure. Despite sin, God gave him clothes and sent him on a journey. Sleep is not missing in Genesis either. Adam slept in the Garden of Eden before the fall.

But even before we get to Adam and Eve, we learn about a God who rests. We have already talked about a God who works, but we also learn that after God completed the heavens and the earth in their entire vast array, God rested. In our work we need to reflect the God who works. In our rest, we must reflect the God who rests.

When we read the first chapter of Genesis, we see that the seventh day is unusual. The account of creation in Genesis is told through the structure of a week. We are told that each day has an evening and a morning. (Not morning and then evening as we may expect. Rest seems to be central to the pattern. This is why the Jewish Sabbath begins on Friday evening.) However on the seventh day we are not told that there is an evening and a morning. There is no close to the day. God's rest seemingly has no end: God's rest is our history.

God did not rest from working – we saw in chapter 3 that God never stops working at sustaining the universe. God did not rest because he was tired, had run out of energy, or because he needed a breather. God rested from creating because he wanted to admire and enjoy his finished work, and because he wanted to set a pattern for human work. God models in his own behavior that work is not ultimate, or obsessive or never-ending, but is to be balanced by rest and reflection on the goodness of the creation.

Sleeping tablet

God not only models this pattern, he specifically states it as one of the ten most important rules for communal life, and tells Moses to inscribe it on tablets of stone at Mount Sinai.

> Remember the Sabbath day by keeping it holy. Six days you shall labor and do all your work, but the seventh day is a Sabbath to the LORD your God. On it you shall not do any work, neither you, nor your son or daughter, nor your manservant or maidservant, nor your animals, nor the alien within your gates. For in six days the LORD made the heavens and the earth, the sea, and all that is in them, but he rested on the seventh day. Therefore the LORD blessed the Sabbath day and made it holy (Exod. 20:8-11).

There are three main implications of this. Firstly, God wanted to ensure that his people were following his rhythm, setting them apart from the nations around them. Secondly, God wanted to make sure that his people were trusting him. In a culture that relied on agriculture as its main industry, it must have been hard to take a day off from planting or harvesting. It was a risk to their crops and their income. We can empathise – in a culture that believes in shopping seven days of the week, it is hard to take a day off. Thirdly, God asked his people to protect the rest day not only for their own benefit, but for the benefit of those around them. We need to help others to achieve an appropriate rhythm to their lives. We can help our families, our employees and our society as we protect and promote rest.

Church ministers find it very hard to support the Keep Sunday Special campaign, as they work on Sundays. As a pastor I used to take Saturdays as my day of rest. When I used to walk to my office early on Sunday mornings to get ready for the day's services, I went past an Anglican church with a large bell tower. Before I would notice it, I found my steps synchronising with the chimes of the bell. The rhythm subconsciously affected my pace and so a campanologist that I had never met set the rhythm for my stride. It was hard work to avoid being caught by the rhythm. I felt like a child following the Pied Piper of Hamlyn with his irresistible music. God set a "six plus one" rhythm for our life and yet the beat of our culture is so strong that it often captures us and breaks us away from our most precious relationships.

Fast asleep

The beat of our culture seems to be speeding up all the time, sweeping us all along in its pace of life. I am sure McDonald's plays fast-paced music in order to force us to eat our fast food at record speed. At home I use labor-saving devices to manage my busy life: I order my food on the internet, cook it in the microwave and then wash the dishes on the quick cycle of my dishwasher. I am constantly upgrading my computer or my computer internet connection to download more information faster. When I am at the end of my tether with the stress of the motion sickness I experience as life hurtles along at a frantic pace, I go to my local chemist and what does he give me – a "fast-acting" headache pill. In our fast-paced culture, we even have a new concept in sleep: the power-nap. Some believe a short sharp burst of sleep will manage to re-energise our bodies sufficiently for us to keep going. But a-fast-sleep is no substitute for fast-a-sleep, the way God designed us to rest.

When we live the rat race, time is very precious, time is money. This affects our home life as well as our work life. Britain has the longest working hours of any country in Europe and it is taking its toll. In a recent survey of managers 87% said that they had no time for other interests. 71% said that this lack of time for personal leisure was damaging their health and 86% said it was damaging relationships with their spouse and children.[1] According to Lord Winston only a minority of dads spend an hour of time with their children each day.

When I was nine years old, I went on a school trip to Pevensey Castle. While we were exploring the grounds we spotted a rope swing. I decided to run full pelt down a little hill to get to the swing. I gave it all I'd got and was straining every muscle in my body to get there first. Half way down the hill I realised that I could not stop – the momentum was too much to compensate for and so, in front of my entire class, I went flying into the moat, an embarrassment I never lived down at that school.

Does the speed of life that we operate at every day mean that we can't actually stop? Do we even know what rest is? When we are out of control and rushing everything, life zooms past us and we don't have time to smell the roses. We need to get out of the rat race, consciously say no to the beat that our work life and the media are imposing on us, and listen to God's rhythm for our life.

For most of us today, the only way we stop is if our bodies force us to. Repetitive Strain Injury or Irritable Bowel Syndrome are often brought on by too much work and stress. Other symptoms of lack of rest include headaches, migraine, raised blood pressure and psoriasis and of course stress-related conditions can be self-perpetuating, as being ill is sometimes more stressful than restful.

When God set a rhythm of six days work and one day of rest in Genesis, he had to reiterate it in the Ten Commandments. But by the time Jesus was on the scene there needed to be another reminder. Jesus had to check those who had become so legalistic about Sabbath keeping, that they had forgotten why God had given it to them in the first place. The Pharisees might have forbidden work, but they had forgotten that stress was not conducive to God-given rest. Adding rules to be kept on the Sabbath, such as how many steps could or could not be taken, was burdening the people. Jesus challenged that attitude while upholding the benefits of the seventh day of rest. "Sabbath was made for man, not man for the Sabbath" (Mark 2:27). God's command to take a day of rest was a gift for our welfare. The disciples took the bold step not of destroying the Sabbath, but of moving it to a Sunday to move away from the Jewish ritual and to celebrate the resurrection of Jesus; the new creation that God started in raising Jesus from the dead.

Taking time off from work says to the world around that God sets the rhythm of our life. It says that work, productivity and money-making do not ultimately drive us. Taking time out to rest proclaims that we were made for God's pleasure and to enjoy God. When the Bible says that God made the Sabbath day holy, it means he set it apart for his purposes. That does not mean we should have a "Give God Sunday and then do whatever you like on Monday" attitude. It means that we can live for God every day.

Sleeping like a baby

This rhythm of work and rest should be reflected not just in the shape of our weeks but also in our daily experience too. Giving proper time for sleep is a sign of faith. Sleep may seem like a waste of time. When we only have on average

600,000 hours of life why would we want to waste 200,000 of them unconscious? There are so many things to pack into life: so much to do, yet so little time. When we feel that we should be busy, or we ought to be worrying, sleep is a declaration of faith.

Think of the picture of Jesus in the boat in a storm so severe that even experienced fishermen are terrified for their lives. Jesus is asleep in the boat, happily resting in the watching care of his Father God. When we rest, and when we sleep, we trust God that he is in control. Whatever the buffeting circumstances of life throw at us, we can fall asleep in God's watchful care. We can be like children falling asleep in our parents' arms. What a comfort it is to know that God never sleeps. He is in control during the dark nights. He is in control during the dangerous storms. Taking a regular day off and sleeping the proper amount of hours in a day is a powerful sign of faith in our God.

There are things that prevent us from sleeping. Environmental and physical factors can keep us awake for short or long periods of time. Noisy neighbors, a bright streetlight or our children's habits keep many of us awake night after night. Sometimes we suffer sleep disorders as a result of our own bodies breaking down. Since God made sleep to be as essential to us as food, air and water, we have the freedom to ask God for sleep, just as we ask him for our daily bread or physical healing. People suffering, often invisibly, from insomnia or other sleep disorders should feel no shame in gathering people around to pray for them. It may not be an illness, and it may not be life-threatening, but it is distressing and frustrating, and it is not how God intended life to be.

There can also be spiritual factors that affect how well we sleep. Sometimes our consciences torment us, and without the distractions of the daytime, they plague us at night. An Indian proverb goes: "The softest pillow is a clear conscience." The Bible puts it in the negative – "There is no rest for the wicked" (Isa. 57:21), and commands us not to let the sun go down on our anger (Eph. 4:26). God has given us consciences deliberately to provoke us to call out to him, day or night. When we have a missing peace because of an argument or failure, or because we have let people down at work, we are to bring these things and their consequences before the God who is in complete control over the universe. God's forgiveness is a powerful healer of these types of sleep inhibitors.

Another factor causing lack of sleep is our own minds. The night before I first spoke on this topic at my church, I was lying awake worrying about an evangelistic outreach event that had been banned by our local council. I felt a hypocrite, knowing that I was going to be speaking about trusting God while we sleep the next day. I asked God for peace of mind and put my trust in him for that event. The phobias that grow larger in the night, the concerns for the future, the tasks that need to get done the next day need to be put to one side as we trust God before going to sleep.

When I was nineteen, I felt a huge burden for the non-believing world. I knew that Jesus was the only way the friends and strangers around me would avoid God's just punishment. I used to tell everyone I could about my Savior, but as I traveled on trains or walked through the streets of Brighton, I felt overwhelmed with the responsibility. I considered T-shirts, loud-speakers, and placards. I considered never working. I seriously considered not sleeping, just to help tell the world the gospel. I felt that I was going crazy with the weight of the burden. God spoke to me very clearly at that time. He told me that he had given me enough time to do everything he asked of me. Although I needed to take up the yoke of following Jesus and sharing the good news – in his compassion, he promised me that his yoke was easy and his burden was light (Matt. 11:30).

My relief was profound. I still had the responsibility to share the gospel with the world, but I also understood that my responsibility was limited and that God was in control. I could sleep in peace because time was not scarce; it was divinely measured so that there was enough of it to do everything he had given me to do. And God had designed me, for a certain amount of time each day, to sleep. It may not always feel like it – but everyone has twenty-four hours in a day, whether a baby or a businessman, a prime minister or a parent. We need to grasp hold of the fact that we all have exactly enough time to do all that God has called us to do.

While you were sleeping

I was also relieved that my sleeping time was not wasted time in God's economics as I read the stories of the Bible. The Bible is full of examples of people who encounter God while they are sleeping: Abimelech, Jacob, Joseph, Egyptian prisoners, Pharaoh, Solomon, Nebuchadnezzar, the other Joseph, the wise men, and Pilate's wife. God prepares, directs, warns and challenges people through their dreams. Our God is a God who can speak to us day and night – a truth also declared by the Psalmists (Ps. 1:3, Ps. 16:7).

Although I struggled for a while on an insufficient amount of sleep, I also have to admit to occasionally struggling with the equal and opposite temptation, and that is to sleep too much. The Bible warns us in Proverbs about prizing sleep too highly, which can lead to laziness. "How long will you lie there, you sluggard? When will you get up from your sleep? A little sleep, a little slumber, a little folding of the hands to rest – and poverty will come on you like a bandit and scarcity like an armed man" (Prov. 6:9-11).

Jesus was not the only person to fall asleep in a boat in a storm. Jonah also had to be awakened in a storm by frightened sailors. But his sleep was not the sleep of someone who was trusting in God's care. His sleep was a means of escape from what he was supposed to be doing. It was an attempt to block out God's voice and God's calling. We need to be careful not to sleep too much, and in so doing becoming too lazy to do what God wants us to do.

Rest in peace

One Bank Holiday we went shopping far too early; the shops were still shut, there was nowhere to go. We walked around for a long while, but it was cold and we just wanted to sit down. There was only one place on the High Street that was open. We had to work very hard at making that McDonald's breakfast meal stretch from its usual seven minutes consumption time to a whole hour. That morning we felt briefly homeless. We experienced a tiny taste of what it is like when there is nowhere to go and nowhere to rest.

Once they were thrown out of the Garden of Eden the people of God were homeless; they longed for a place of rest, and so God promised them the Promised Land. It was to be a place of rest from their wanderings and from their enemies, a place where even food and drink was handed to them on a plate: a land flowing with milk and honey. But the Promised Land was also a picture to help us understand what heaven is going to be like. God is preparing for us a place of rest. This truth that spans the whole Bible has three main implications for us.

Firstly, we see rest as ultimately fulfilled in heaven. When God's people rebelled against him in the desert, and God promised that they would never enter his rest, he meant that they would not enter the Promised Land. But when the writer to the Hebrews refers to this incident in chapter 3, telling us to "make every effort to enter the rest", he applies this Old Testament passage to our response to Christ. If we trust Christ till the end then we will enter God's ultimate rest, but if we don't then we will be prevented from entering the rest of heaven because of our unbelief.

Secondly, we see "preparing rest" as a godly characteristic. We can be like God in this respect when we offer rest to people around us who need it. Whether this is supporting the local hospice or shelter or sending money, blankets or Christmas shoeboxes to the destitute around the world, we can appreciate the privilege of joining in God's work. As we ensure that the people we work with are not overworking or as we are hospitable to neighbors, families and strangers, we are giving people a foretaste of heaven, and we should be grateful to God for this privilege of being like him.

Thirdly, this picture of rest and heaven should transform the way we consider death. Death is not the end, but is the beginning of our eternal rest with God. As we offer needy people the chance to rest physically, we also need to find ways to help people know how they can enjoy the security of resting in peace with God. The physical tiredness we experience can be a way of remembering that we were made for the spiritual rest that comes from knowing God. It is a reminder to us in our bodies that we long for heaven. The only way to gain this permanent, satisfying rest is by trusting in the work that Jesus did on the cross; the work that Jesus finished on the cross. Augustine famously put it:[2] "Our hearts are restless until they find their rest in thee." When we have found this rest for ourselves, we need to bring others into it.

The Bible uses the word sleep as a metaphor for death in 1 Corinthians 15 where Paul encourages the church with his teaching on death and resurrection: "But Christ has indeed been raised from the dead, the firstfruits of those who have fallen asleep. We will not all sleep, but we will all be changed – in a flash, in the twinkling of an eye, at the last trumpet" (verses 20 and 52). For those of us who fear death, the image of death as sleep gives us great comfort. Jesus is able to raise people from the dead as easily as rousing someone from sleep. When Jesus faces the screams of the bereaved in Jairus' house, he says "Why all this commotion and wailing? The child is not dead but asleep" (Mark 5:39). This is taste of things to come. One day Christ will awaken all those who have trusted in him. We can trust Jesus will wake us up in time.

Just a minute

What are you going to do with the rest of your life? Here are some practical suggestions. Adopt God's rhythm of work and rest, day and night, six days + one day. And when you finish work for the day, or for the week, do something practical to state your trust in him. Set a curfew and put the hoover out of sight, leave your laptop at work, leave your revision to one side.

Critically evaluate the pace of your life. Fight against the rhythm of the world by taking your coffee breaks, eating your meal at a table, relaxing.

Be like God and bring rest to other people. The Ten Commandments as recorded in Deuteronomy extended the Sabbath to the servants and animals, mirroring the compassion of God. Encourage your employees to leave their work behind on Friday night, campaign for fair working hours and a balanced working week. Respect the good neighbor rule of quiet after 11.00 p.m. Help out those who are sleep deprived by taking the pressure off.

Read yourself a bedtime story, and what better story than the story of God himself as he deals with his people? Memorise some verses so you can meditate on God's word day and night, asking God himself to instruct you as you sleep.

On the iPod

Day Sleeper, R.E.M. (Warner Bros, 1998)
Don't Dream It's Over, Crowded House (Capitol Rec., 1986)
Abide With Me, Henry Lyte (1847)
The Lord's My Shepherd, Stuart Townend (Kingsway Music, 1996)
Stand By Me, Ben E. King (ATCO Records, 1961)

Off the shelf

St. John of the Cross, *Dark Night of the Soul* (Dover: Dover Publications, 2003)
Philip K. Dick, *Do Androids Dream of Electric Sheep* (London: Orion, 2005)
John Piper, *Don't Waste Your Life* (Wheaton: Crossway, 2005)

Notes

[1] "Quality of working life" – 1999 survey of managers changing experiences, Les Worrall and Cary Cooper, Institute of Management, quoted in Mark Greene, *Thank God It's Monday* (Bletchley: Scripture Union, 2001).

[2] W.H. Hutchings Trans. (1883), *Confessions of St. Augustine* (London: Rivingtons, 1883), p.1.

LIGHTS OUT

Lights out

Hopefully you haven't fallen asleep reading the last chapter. At the beginning of this book, I introduced you to one of my heroes: Jack Bauer from the television show *24*. Unfortunately Jack Bauer is the sort of hero that makes me feel completely inadequate. What's all in a days work for Jack is more than the sum total of my entire life.

Through the chapters of this book, I have introduced you to my true aspiration. I hope that you have seen that every moment of our lives can be invested with significance, full of opportunities to demonstrate to God that he really is our number one hero. We can honor God in our battle with greed at the fridge door. We can worship God as we relate to carers at the school gate. We can show our love for God as we control ourselves in the traffic jam. We can reflect God to others as we visit elderly and infirm friends and relatives. Every second counts for God in our lives of worship.

I hope that through this book you have been given a bigger picture of what it means to live full-time for Christ, and what it means to worship him. Can you imagine the difference it would make if we all lived every day as Christ has called us to? No longer would we be able to maintain an outward show of spirituality when our hearts are untransformed. No longer would the world be able to accuse the church of hypocrisy.

Integrating our faith into everyday living: this is the only way that we can honor the God who deserves our allegiance in every facet of our lives. It is the only way that a watching world will see the truth of the gospel lived out in front of it. In a world that hungers for authenticity, integrated worship is needed.

As we turn the lights out at the end of this book, my prayer is that it will turn a light on inside your heart as you consider how to worship God with your next twenty-four hours. It is my hope that it will send you out as lights in a dark world to shine for our King.